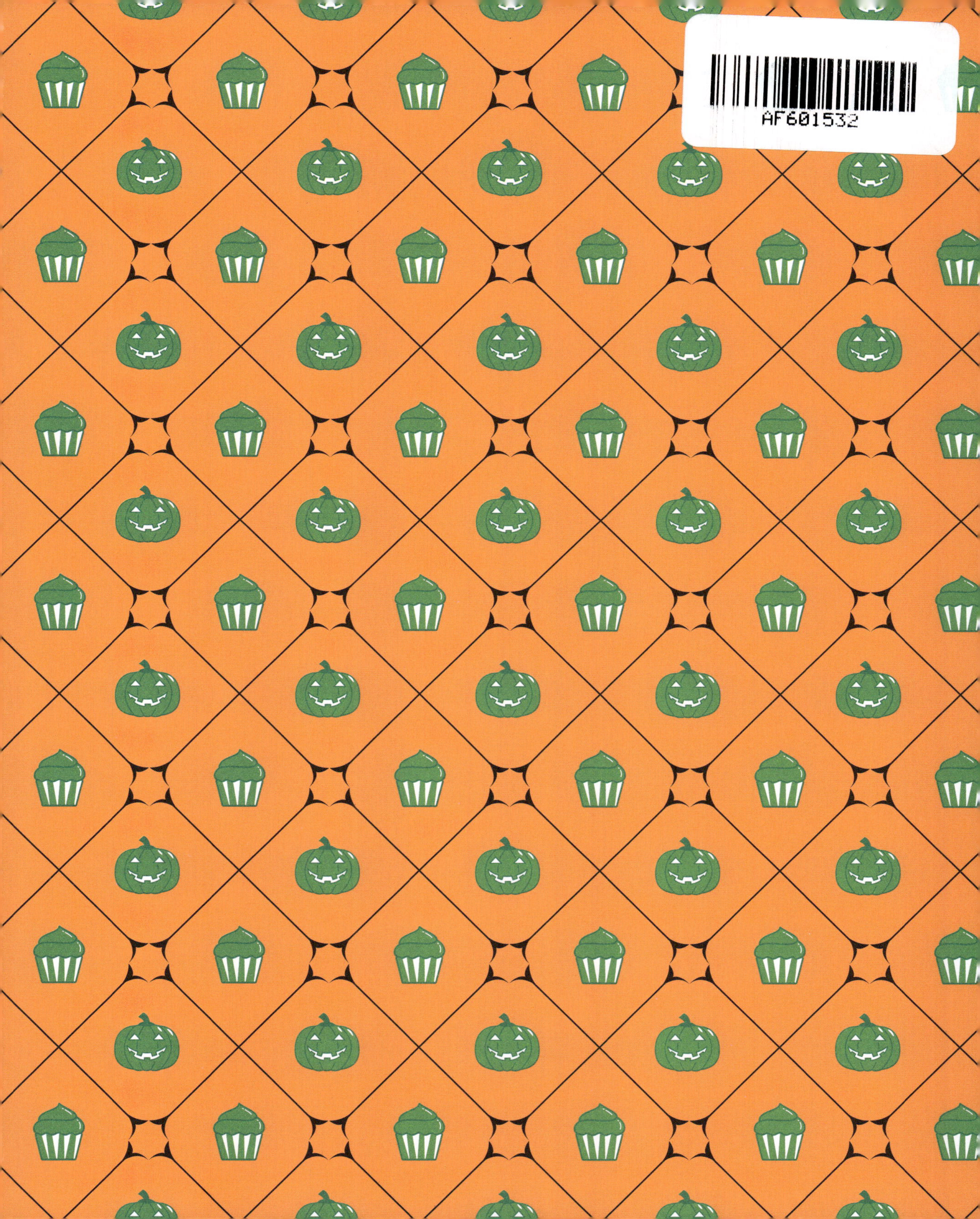

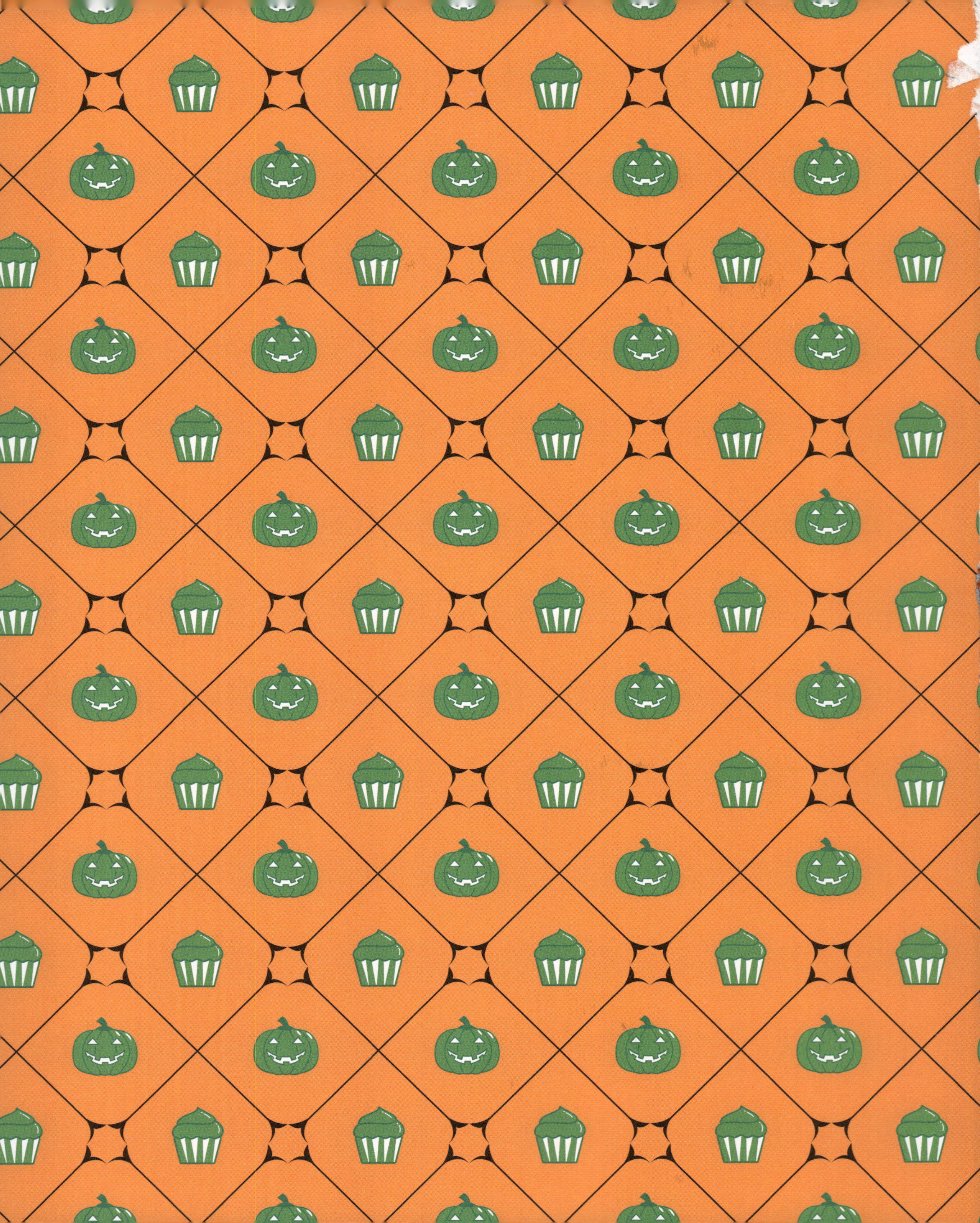

THE
HALLOWEEN
MOVIE
COOKBOOK

SIMON ELEMENT

New York Amsterdam/Antwerp London Toronto Sydney/Melbourne New Delhi

THE HALLOWEEN MOVIE COOKBOOK

65 Hauntingly Delicious Recipes Inspired by Your Favorite Spooky Movies

Ryan Alvarez and Adam Merrin

CREATORS OF HUSBANDS THAT COOK

CONTENTS

MOVIE

A NIGHTMARE ON ELM STREET
(1984)

BEETLEJUICE
(1988)

CASPER
(1995)

CHILD'S PLAY
(1988)

COCO
(2017)

CORALINE
(2009)

CORPSE BRIDE
(2005)

DEATH BECOMES HER
(1992)

FRIGHT NIGHT
(1985)

GHOSTBUSTERS
(1984)

HALLOWEEN
(1978)

HALLOWEENTOWN
(1998)

HOCUS POCUS
(1993)

INTERVIEW WITH THE VAMPIRE
(1994)

IT
(2017)

IT'S THE GREAT PUMPKIN, CHARLIE BROWN
(1966)

LIST

(IN ALPHABETICAL ORDER)

NIGHT OF THE LIVING DEAD
(1968)

PRACTICAL MAGIC
(1998)

SCREAM
(1996)

SLEEPY HOLLOW
(1999)

THE ADDAMS FAMILY
(1991)

THE CRAFT
(1996)

THE EVIL DEAD
(1981)

THE HAUNTED MANSION
(2003)

THE LOST BOYS
(1987)

THE NIGHTMARE BEFORE CHRISTMAS
(1993)

THE ROCKY HORROR PICTURE SHOW
(1975)

THE SHINING
(1980)

THE SIXTH SENSE
(1999)

THE WITCHES
(1990)

THE WITCHES OF EASTWICK
(1987)

INTRODUCTION

Welcome, foolish mortals, to *The Halloween Movie Cookbook*. We are your hosts. Your *ghost hosts*. Kindly dim the lights and set your candles aglow. There's no turning back now.

(THUNDER CLAPS. LIGHTS GO OUT. SOMEONE SCREAMS.)

If you're the type who loves watching spooky films all year long—not just in October—this book is for you. We've consulted the spirits and conjured up sixty-five spine-chilling recipes, potions, and spells inspired by thirty-one classic Halloween movies, from Bewitching Breakfasts and Spooky Snacks and Sides to Monstrous Mains and Devilish Desserts. Whether you're preparing a platter of Dead Man's Toes (page 64) from **HOCUS POCUS** for a quick nibble or baking a double batch of Tally Me Banana Cupcakes (page 149) for a **BEETLEJUICE**-themed party, there are tricks and treats for every occasion.

Have you ever wished you could join the Midnight Margaritas (page 138) party in **PRACTICAL MAGIC**? Have you ever wondered what those levitating pancakes (see page 27) taste like in **CASPER**? Have you ever wanted to make your own glowing pink Potion of Eternal Youth (page 117) like in **DEATH BECOMES HER**? Well, now you can!

Join us for a fang-tastic food tour where sadistic clowns, killer dolls, and masked murderers lurk around every corner. Pack your broomstick and bring a crucifix—there are vampires everywhere. You'll stop by the Land of the Dead to learn what the recently deceased like to eat, time warp to Dr. Frank-N-Furter's castle for a fabulous late-night feast, and spend a quiet weekend at the historic Overlook Hotel, where the rum is flowing and the sun is shining. You'll take a trip on a magic flying bus to Halloweentown, and you're cordially invited to a home-cooked meal at the Addams Family residence.

As lifelong devotees of spooky movies, we wrote this book not just for horror lovers, but for anyone who sees Halloween as a year-round state of mind. Whether you're throwing a costume party in July or curling up with a scary flick on a stormy night, these wicked recipes will leave you spellbound.

Sharpen your knives, gather some garlic, and preheat your cauldron—this tour is about to take flight.

Eternally yours,
Ryan and Adam

Caution—this cookbook is not for the faint of heart. If some of these culinary delights are too frightening, check out our previous book, *That Takes the Cookie*, for a . . . gentler read.

LIST OF RECIPES BY MOVIE TITLE

MOVIE LIST BY THEME

Dying to throw a witch-themed party? Are you hosting a vampire ball under the next full moon? Want to celebrate an evening of serial killers with your friends? This section is organized by spooky movie genre to help you plan the perfect themed gathering.

MOVIE LIST IN CHRONOLOGICAL ORDER

Total
Server
0000007
VEG/POT - DESSERT - BEV

SPOOKY MOVIE NIGHT MENU SUGGESTIONS

Hosting a spooky movie night party? Or perhaps you're planning an evening with the ghoul of your dreams and looking for some sinister serving suggestions. These menu ideas for themed parties, dinners, and date nights will get you started and leave your friends screaming for more.

VAMPIRE'S LAIR

Spaghetti and Meatballs with Extra Garlic (*The Lost Boys*) (page 89)

Vampire Blood Negroni (*The Lost Boys*) (page 128)

New Orleans Beignets with Raspberry Coulis (*Interview with the Vampire*) (page 177)

ADDAMS FAMILY FEAST

Entrails on Toast (Wild Mushroom Crostini) (*The Addams Family*) (page 47)

Grandmama's Spécialité de la Maison (Squid Ink Paella) (*The Addams Family*) (page 84)

Wednesday & Pugsley's Poison Lemonade (*The Addams Family*) (page 109)

CREEPY CRAWLY SPREAD

Eyeball Soup (Roasted Tomato Soup with Mozzarella Eyeballs) (*Corpse Bride*) (page 59)

Dead Man's Toes (Pigs in a Blanket) (*Hocus Pocus*) (page 64)

Deceiving Chinese Takeout Noodles with Shiitake Mushroom Worms (*The Lost Boys*) (page 101)

Wednesday & Pugsley's Poison Lemonade (*The Addams Family*) (page 109)

Oogie Boogie Ooey Gooey Green Peanut Butter Chocolate Fudge (*The Nightmare Before Christmas*) (page 181)

WITCHES GATHERING

Slumber Party Artichoke Dip with Gruyère and Spinach (*The Craft*) (page 55)

Dead Man's Toes (Pigs in a Blanket) (*Hocus Pocus*) (page 64)

Crispy Baked Scrod with Lemon and Parmesan (*Hocus Pocus*) (page 94)

Midnight Margaritas with Lime and Coconut (*Practical Magic*) (page 138)

Brownies for Breakfast (*Practical Magic*) (page 187)

EVENING OF THE LIVING DEAD

Eyeball Soup (Roasted Tomato Soup with Mozzarella Eyeballs) (*Corpse Bride*) (page 59)

Entrails on Toast (Wild Mushroom Crostini) (*The Addams Family*) (page 47)

Dead Man's Toes (Pigs in a Blanket) (*Hocus Pocus*) (page 64)

Passionfruit Zombie (*Night of the Living Dead*) (page 131)

Molten Red Chocolate Demon Cakes (*The Evil Dead*) (page 161)

GHOST GALA

Grilled Prawns with a Tarragon-Mustard Dip (*Beetlejuice*) (page 48)

Louis's Smoked Salmon Dip from Nova Scotia (*Ghostbusters*) (page 63)

Lazarus Potion (*Casper*) (page 110)

Attic Cookies (Cinnamon Swirl Snickerdoodles) (*The Haunted Mansion*) (page 175)

KILLER CONVENTION

Flaming Hot Popcorn (*Scream*) (page 75)

Sharp Skewers with Cajun Shrimp and Peppers (*A Nightmare on Elm Street*) (page 102)

Bloodbath Punch (*It*) (page 127)

Headless Gingerbread People (*Sleepy Hollow*) (page 191)

DIA DE LOS MUERTOS FIESTA

Mashed Potato Taquitos (*Coco*) (page 51)

Esquites Mexican Street Corn Salad (*Coco*) (page 52)

Tamales de Rajas con Queso (*Coco*) (page 87)

Apple Cider Churros with Dulce de Leche (*Coco*) (page 155)

Redrum Sangria (*The Shining*) (page 141)

SLUMBER PARTY SNACKS

Slumber Party Artichoke Dip with Gruyère and Spinach (*The Craft*) (page 55)

Flaming Hot Popcorn (*Scream*) (page 75)

Midnight Margaritas with Lime and Coconut (*Practical Magic*) (page 138)

Myers's Meyer Lemon Bars (*Halloween*) (page 172)

LADIES NIGHT

Louis's Smoked Salmon Dip from Nova Scotia (*Ghostbusters*) (page 63)

Louis's Rat-atouille (*Interview with the Vampire*) (page 97)

Ladies' Night Pitcher Martinis (*The Witches of Eastwick*) (page 142)

Madeline's Madeleines (*Death Becomes Her*) (page 165)

SPOOKY MUSICALS PARTY

Sally's Sneaky Roasted Cauliflower Soup with Frog's Breath and Worm's Wart (*The Nightmare Before Christmas*) (page 68)

Hot Potato, Bless My Soul Patatas Bravas with a (Tim) Curry Aïoli (*The Rocky Horror Picture Show*) (page 72)

Crispy Baked Scrod with Lemon and Parmesan (*Hocus Pocus*) (page 94)

Apple Cider Churros with Dulce de Leche (*Coco*) (page 155)

TIM BURTON TRIBUTE

Eyeball Soup (Roasted Tomato Soup with Mozzarella Eyeballs) (*Corpse Bride*) (page 59)

Grilled Prawns with a Tarragon-Mustard Dip (*Beetlejuice*) (page 48)

Katrina's Nighttime Brew (*Sleepy Hollow*) (page 133)

Tally Me Banana Cupcakes (*Beetlejuice*) (page 149)

WITCHES TEA PARTY

Bewitching Raisin Buns (*The Witches*) (page 39)

Cucumber Sandwiches with Butter, Not Margarine (*The Witches*) (page 76)

Hotel Excelsior's Creamy Cress Soup (*The Witches*) (page 79)

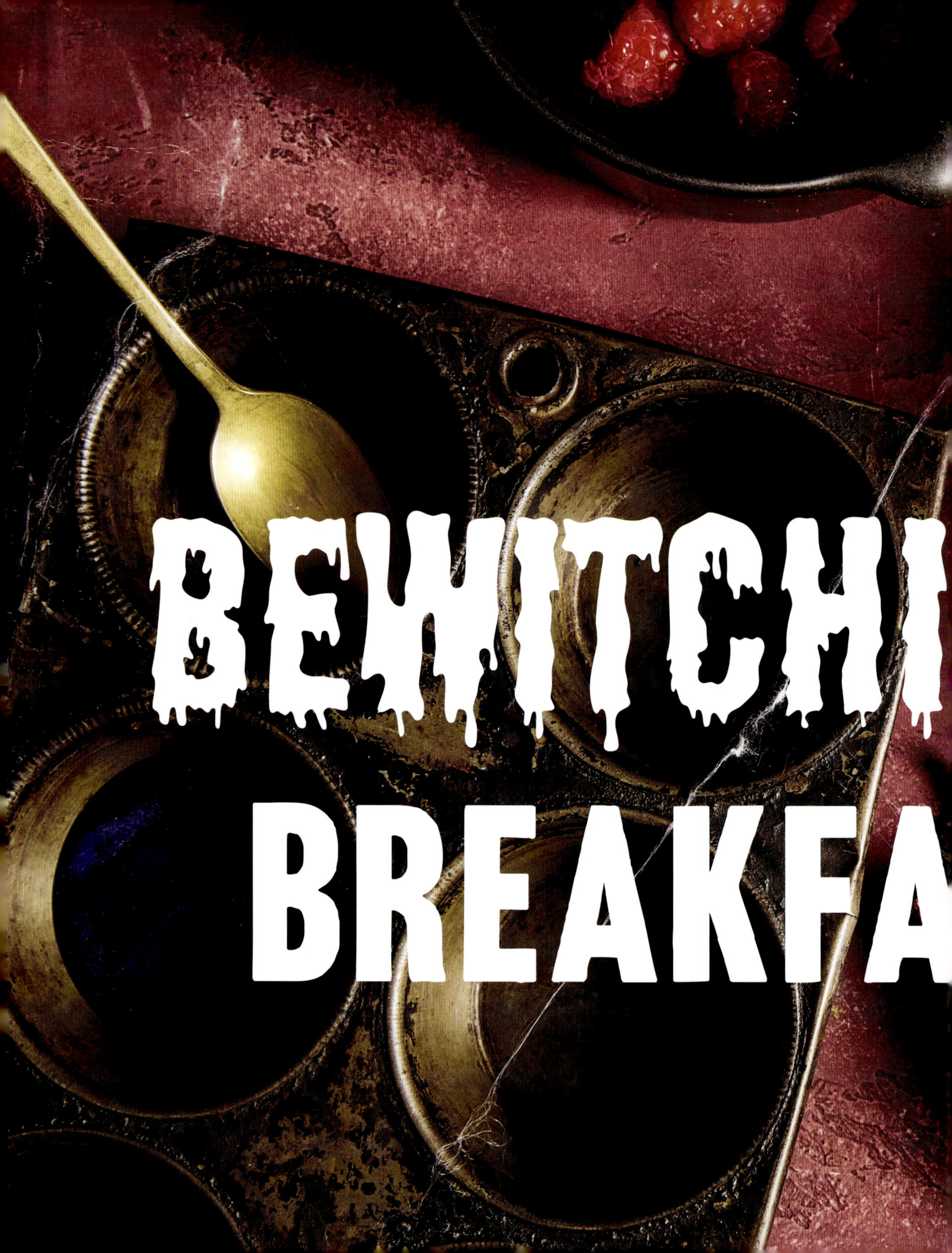
BEWITCHI
BREAKFA

NG
STS

(A DARK AND CLOUDY MORNING. LIGHTNING FLASHES, AND A HEAVY RAIN BEGINS TO POUR.)

Rise and shine and wake the dead! It's important to start the day with a nutritious . . . bite, and this chapter is filled with recipes that are mortally mouthwatering. If you're craving something sweet, bake a batch of The Other Mother's Orange-Blueberry Muffins (page 28) inspired by CORALINE to transport you to another world. Or, if you're seeking something savory, The Overlook Hotel Breakfast Frittata with Jack Cheese (page 36) has been a guest favorite for over one hundred years. Make a cup of coffee, ignore the zombies clawing at your kitchen window, and treat yourself to a Bewitching Breakfast!

"I'm a ghost, yes, I admit it.
But I'm a friendly ghost!"
—CASPER

A TALL STACK OF PUMPKIN PANCAKES

CASPER
(1995)

"Don't scream" when you read the good news: Casper has graciously agreed to share his famous pancake recipe—the same one he prepared for Kat and her dad on their first morning at Whipstaff Manor. Humbly made with cinnamon, ginger, nutmeg, and allspice, these friendly flapjacks taste just like classic pumpkin pie—a class above the Hostess dessert platter devoured by the Ghostly Trio at breakfast. So channel Casper, pour yourself a glass of freshly squeezed orange juice (through your hand, of course), and prepare your palate for pumpkin pancake perfection.

MAKES ABOUT 12 SIX-INCH PANCAKES

- 1½ cups (180 g) all-purpose flour
- ¼ cup (53 g) packed dark brown sugar
- 2 teaspoons baking powder
- 1½ teaspoons ground cinnamon
- 1 teaspoon ground ginger
- 1 teaspoon baking soda
- ½ teaspoon salt
- ½ teaspoon ground nutmeg
- ¼ teaspoon ground allspice
- 1½ cups (355 ml) evaporated milk (not condensed milk)
- 2 large eggs
- 1 cup (226 g) canned pumpkin purée (not pumpkin pie filling)
- 3 tablespoons unsalted butter, melted
- Vegetable oil or butter, for cooking
- Softened butter, for serving (optional)
- Maple syrup, for serving (optional)

1. In a medium bowl, combine the flour, brown sugar, baking powder, cinnamon, ginger, baking soda, salt, nutmeg, and allspice. Whisk together until blended, then set aside.

2. In a large bowl, combine the evaporated milk, eggs, and pumpkin purée. Whisk together until smooth and blended, then slowly add the melted butter while continuing to whisk. Add the flour mixture, and whisk together until no lumps remain and the batter is smooth.

3. Preheat a large skillet over medium-low heat. When hot (see Notes), swirl in about a teaspoon of vegetable oil, and spread it evenly around the skillet. Add ¼ cup of the pancake batter and spread it into an even circle about 6 inches wide. Cook for 1 to 2 minutes, until bubbles form on the top of the pancake and the bottom is golden brown. Then flip the pancake and cook for an additional 1 to 2 minutes, until the bottom is golden brown. Transfer to a serving plate, then repeat the process with the remaining batter. Serve hot, with butter and maple syrup, if desired. Bone Appetit!

NOTES

How to test if the skillet is ready: once the skillet is heated, dip your fingers into a small bowl of water, then flick a few drops onto the surface of the skillet. If the drops don't move, the skillet is too cool and not ready yet. If they immediately evaporate and disappear, the skillet is too hot, so reduce the heat. If the drops sizzle and dance, the skillet is ready to cook.

You will probably adjust the heat as you cook the pancakes. If they brown too quickly, turn the heat down. If they take too long and still look undercooked, turn the heat up.

THE OTHER MOTHER'S ORANGE-BLUEBERRY MUFFINS

CORALINE
(2009)

Why does temptation taste so good? When Coraline crosses into the Other World, the Other Mother entices her to stay by preparing a feast of all her favorite foods. While the Other Mother is manipulative and deceptive, we must admit her cooking is on point. Her irresistible muffins are seductively soft, loaded with plump blueberries, and bursting with orange flavor. Baked with hints of vanilla, these tantalizing treats are dreamlike-delicious and truly out of this world.

MAKES ABOUT 16 MUFFINS

- 2¼ cups (270 g) all-purpose flour
- 2 teaspoons baking powder
- 1 teaspoon baking soda
- 1 teaspoon salt
- 8 tablespoons (1 stick/113 g) unsalted butter, at room temperature
- ½ cup (107 g) packed dark brown sugar
- ½ cup (99 g) granulated sugar
- Grated zest from 1 orange
- 2 large eggs, at room temperature
- 2 teaspoons vanilla extract
- ½ cup (113 g) Greek yogurt
- ½ cup (118 ml) freshly squeezed orange juice (2 to 3 oranges)
- 2 cups (310 g) blueberries, plus more for garnish

1. Preheat the oven to 425°F (218°C) and line two muffin pans with sixteen paper liners.

2. In a medium bowl, combine the flour, baking powder, baking soda, and salt. Whisk together until blended, then set aside.

3. In a large mixing bowl, using an electric mixer, beat the butter, brown sugar, granulated sugar, and orange zest on medium speed until light and fluffy. Add the eggs and vanilla and beat until smooth. Add the yogurt and orange juice and beat until blended. Add the flour mixture and beat until no dry streaks remain. Add the blueberries and stir by hand using a silicone spatula, until evenly distributed in the batter.

4. Fill the prepared muffin pans with batter until they are nearly full, then place a few blueberries on top of each one for garnish. Bake for 5 minutes at 425°F (218°C), then reduce the temperature to 350°F (177°C) without opening the oven door. Continue baking for 15 to 20 minutes, until the tops of the muffins are golden brown and a toothpick inserted into the center of a muffin comes out clean with a few moist crumbs sticking to it. If baking two pans at once, swap the positions of the pans halfway through to ensure the muffins bake evenly. Let the muffins cool in the pan for 10 minutes, then transfer to a rack to cool completely. Bone Appetit!

"You could stay here forever.
If you want to."
—THE OTHER MOTHER

"I looove dinner-breakfast-food!"
—THE OTHER FATHER

OTHER WORLD WAFFLES WITH STRAWBERRY SAUCE

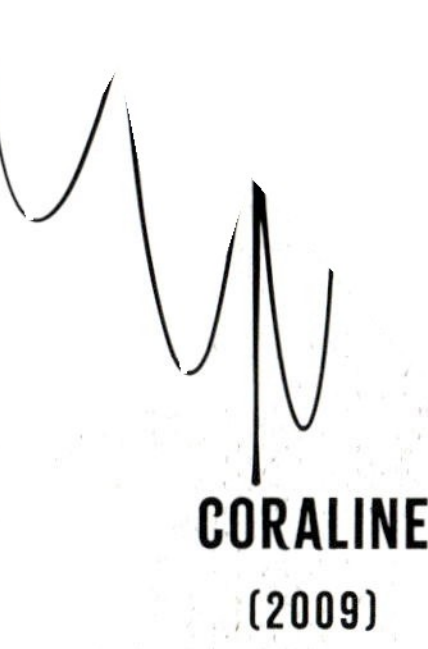

CORALINE
(2009)

Coraline's real father is a notoriously terrible cook. Thankfully, this recipe isn't his. These welcoming waffles from the Other World are a breakfast dream come true—even if the Other Parents serve them at night for "dinner-breakfast-food." With a golden, crisp exterior and a light, fluffy center, these scrumptious squares are drizzled with a sweet strawberry sauce and topped with clouds of whipped cream. Your mornings (or evenings) will never be the same.

MAKES ABOUT 10 SIX-INCH WAFFLES

FOR THE STRAWBERRY SAUCE

- 1 pound (454 g) fresh or frozen strawberries, diced
- ¼ cup (50 g) granulated sugar
- 2 teaspoons vanilla extract
- 2 teaspoons freshly squeezed lemon juice

FOR THE WAFFLES

- 2 cups (240 g) all-purpose flour
- ¼ cup (50 g) granulated sugar
- 3 teaspoons baking powder
- 1 teaspoon salt
- 1½ cups (355 ml) milk of choice
- 3 large eggs
- 2 teaspoons vanilla extract
- 6 tablespoons (86 g) unsalted butter, melted
- Cooking spray, optional
- Whipped cream, homemade (see page 183) or store-bought, for serving
- Fresh hulled strawberries, for serving

1. **MAKE THE STRAWBERRY SAUCE:** In a medium saucepan, combine the strawberries, sugar, vanilla, and lemon juice. Bring to a simmer over medium heat and cook for 8 to 10 minutes, stirring often, until softened. Purée using an immersion blender, potato masher, blender, or food processor. Set aside.

2. **MAKE THE WAFFLES:** In a medium bowl, whisk together the flour, sugar, baking powder, and salt until blended, then set aside.

3. In a large bowl, combine the milk, eggs, and vanilla and whisk together until smooth. While whisking, slowly add the butter. Add the flour mixture and whisk together until smooth with no lumps remaining.

4. Preheat a waffle iron according to the manufacturer's instructions. If needed, lightly coat the iron with cooking spray to prevent sticking.

5. Add batter until the iron is filled—about ¾ cup of batter for each 6-inch-square waffle. Cook for 3 to 5 minutes, depending on the waffle iron, until deeply golden and crisp. Serve immediately topped with the strawberry sauce, whipped cream, and fresh strawberries. Bone Appetit!

HARRIET'S APPLE-CINNAMON MUFFINS FOR THE HEADLESS SHELTER

HALLOWEENTOWN
(1998)

In Halloweentown, witches, goblins, and ghosts all live together in harmony. Harriet, one of the local residents, bumps into Aggie while on the way to the Headless Shelter to donate a basket of muffins. Baked with Granny Smith apples, cinnamon, and apple cider, and topped with a crunchy brown sugar–cinnamon crumble, these perfect pastries bring all the goblins to the yard.

MAKES ABOUT 16 MUFFINS

FOR THE CRUMBLE TOPPING

- ½ cup (60 g) all-purpose flour
- ¼ cup (54 g) packed dark brown sugar
- ¼ cup (50 g) granulated sugar
- 1 teaspoon ground cinnamon
- 4 tablespoons (½ stick/57 g) cold unsalted butter, cubed

FOR THE MUFFINS

- 1¾ cups (210 g) all-purpose flour
- 1½ teaspoons ground cinnamon
- 1 teaspoon baking soda
- 1 teaspoon baking powder
- ½ teaspoon salt
- 8 tablespoons (1 stick/113 g) unsalted butter, at room temperature
- ½ cup (107 g) packed dark brown sugar
- ½ cup (99 g) granulated sugar
- 2 large eggs, at room temperature
- ¼ cup (59 ml) milk of choice
- ¼ cup (59 ml) unfiltered apple juice
- 2 teaspoons vanilla extract
- 2 cups (250 g) peeled and diced Granny Smith apples (about 2 apples)

1 Preheat the oven to 425°F (218°C) and line two muffin pans with sixteen paper liners.

2 **MAKE THE CRUMBLE TOPPING:** In a medium bowl, combine the flour, brown sugar, granulated sugar, and cinnamon. Whisk together until blended, then add the butter, using your fingers to work the butter into the flour mixture until it becomes crumbly and sandy-textured. Set aside.

3 **MAKE THE MUFFINS:** In a medium bowl, combine the flour, cinnamon, baking soda, baking powder, and salt. Whisk together until blended, then set aside.

4 In a large mixing bowl, using an electric mixer, beat the butter, brown sugar, and granulated sugar on medium speed until light and fluffy. Add the eggs and beat until blended. Add the milk, apple juice, and vanilla and beat until smooth. Add the flour mixture and beat until no dry streaks remain. Add the apples and stir by hand using a silicone spatula until evenly distributed in the batter.

5 Use a spoon to fill the prepared muffin cups with batter until they are nearly full, then sprinkle each one with a generous layer of crumble topping. Bake for 5 minutes at 425°F (218°C), then reduce the temperature to 350°F (177°C) without opening the oven door. Continue baking for 15 to 20 minutes, until the tops of the muffins are golden brown and a toothpick inserted into the center of a muffin comes out clean with a few moist crumbs sticking to it. If baking two pans at once, swap the positions of the pans halfway through to ensure the muffins bake evenly. Let the muffins cool in the pan for 10 minutes, then transfer to a rack to cool completely. Bone Appetit!

"Care for a muffin?
I baked 'em for the folks
at the Headless Shelter.
Didn't occur to me that
they couldn't eat them.
No heads!"
—HARRIET

"Life's no fun without a good scare."
—THE RESIDENTS OF HALLOWEEN TOWN

JACK'S BREAKFAST SHAK-SPOOK-A

The sun never rises in Halloween Town, but a ghoul's gotta eat. Shakshuka is a comforting North African dish where eggs are poached in a simmering sauce of tomatoes, peppers, and herbs. For a savory breakfast, Jack Skellington used his savvy skeleton skills in the kitchen to turn this Mediterranean classic into a Halloween Town morning ritual. Intensely aromatic and topped with spooky black olive eyes, this beastly breakfast will scare your morning blues away.

SERVES 3 TO 4

- 1 (28-ounce/794 g) can whole peeled Italian tomatoes
- 2 tablespoons extra-virgin olive oil
- 1 green bell pepper (120 g), thinly sliced
- 2 large garlic cloves (10 g), finely chopped
- ¼ cup (59 ml) dry red wine, such as Pinot Noir, Merlot, or Chianti
- 1 tablespoon unsalted butter
- 1¼ teaspoons salt
- ½ teaspoon granulated sugar
- ⅛ teaspoon red pepper flakes
- 1 sprig fresh rosemary
- 6 large eggs
- Black olives, sliced, for garnish
- Crumbled feta cheese, for garnish
- Fresh Italian parsley, finely chopped, for garnish
- Crusty slices of bread or toast, for serving (optional)

1. Open the can of tomatoes and pour all the contents into a medium bowl. Use your hands to squeeze and crush the tomatoes, breaking them apart into pieces to create a chunky purée. Set aside.

2. Place a large skillet (approximately 12 inches/30 cm) over medium heat. When the skillet is hot (see Notes, page 27), swirl in the olive oil. Add the bell pepper and cook for 5 to 7 minutes, stirring occasionally, until softened. Then add the garlic and cook for 1 minute. Add the crushed tomatoes, wine, butter, salt, sugar, red pepper flakes, and rosemary and stir to combine. Raise the heat to medium-high to bring to a boil. Once boiling, reduce the heat and simmer for 15 minutes uncovered, stirring occasionally.

3. Carefully remove the rosemary sprig, then crack the eggs into the skillet, arranging them evenly and leaving space between each one. Cover the skillet and cook for about 2½ minutes, or until the whites of the eggs are fully cooked and no longer transparent.

4. Before serving, place 2 olive slices on each egg to resemble eyes, and garnish the skillet with feta cheese and parsley. Serve immediately, with slices of bread for dipping, if desired. Bone Appetit!

THE OVERLOOK HOTEL BREAKFAST FRITTATA WITH JACK CHEESE

THE SHINING

(1980)

Your weekend getaway at the Overlook Hotel wouldn't be complete without trying their famous breakfast frittata. It's been a staple at the luxury resort since its opening in 1910. Created by one of the hotel's first winter caretakers, the now-fabled omelet has remained on the menu ever since. Baked with sautéed broccoli, red bell pepper, zucchini, mushrooms, and cherry tomatoes, this colorful concoction will keep the sun shining on a blizzardy day. Loaded with melty Monterey Jack cheese and topped with sliced scallions, you'll soon understand why this treasured dish has been part of the Overlook family for more than a century—without getting the axe.

SERVES 4 TO 6

- 8 large eggs
- ½ cup (118 ml) whole milk
- 1½ teaspoons salt, divided
- ¼ teaspoon freshly ground black pepper
- ⅛ teaspoon red pepper flakes
- 1 cup (113 g) shredded Monterey Jack cheese, divided
- 2 tablespoons extra-virgin olive oil
- ½ cup (65 g) chopped yellow onion
- 2 large garlic cloves (10 g), finely chopped
- ⅔ cup (95 g) chopped red bell pepper (about 1 pepper)
- ⅔ cup (50 g) chopped broccoli florets (about 1 small head)
- ⅔ cup (95 g) chopped zucchini (about 1 zucchini)
- ⅔ cup (60 g) chopped mushrooms (4 to 5 mushrooms)
- ⅔ cup (105 g) halved cherry tomatoes (10 to 12 tomatoes), plus more for garnish
- Sliced scallions, for garnish

1. Preheat the oven to 350°F (177°C).

2. In a large bowl, combine the eggs, milk, ¾ teaspoon of the salt, the black pepper, and red pepper flakes. Whisk together until smooth and evenly blended. Add ¾ cup of the cheese and whisk together until combined. Set aside.

3. Place a 12-inch oven-safe skillet over medium heat. When the skillet is hot (see Notes, page 27), swirl in the olive oil. Add the onion and cook for 5 to 7 minutes, stirring occasionally, until softened. Add the garlic and cook for 1 minute. Add the bell pepper, broccoli, zucchini, mushrooms, cherry tomatoes, and the remaining ¾ teaspoon of salt, then stir to combine. Cook for 6 to 8 minutes, stirring occasionally, until the vegetables are softened. Add the egg mixture and stir briefly to distribute the vegetables in an even layer. Cook without stirring for 2 to 3 minutes, until the edges just begin to set. Garnish with a few halved cherry tomatoes evenly across the surface, then top with the remaining ¼ cup of cheese.

4. Transfer the skillet to the oven and bake for 15 to 20 minutes, until the center is set and no longer liquid. Let the skillet cool for 10 minutes, then top with sliced scallions and serve. Bone Appetit!

"This is one of the finest resorts in America. A place people come to for peace and quiet."

—STUART ULLMAN

“The raisins are all ’round
the edge of these cakes.
They’re really good!”
—BRUNO JENKINS

BEWITCHING RAISIN BUNS

THE WITCHES
(1990)

The golden raisin buns at the grand Hotel Excelsior are so irresistible that Bruno Jenkins couldn't wait until they were served, sneaking into the hotel's banquet room to pick raisins off the buns when no one was looking. Thankfully, you won't have to travel to the English seaside or deal with a wicked witch convention to enjoy these pillow-soft buns. Delicately spiced with cinnamon, these buttery rolls are filled with plump, vanilla-soaked raisins. Served warm with butter and a drizzle of honey, we promise we won't tell if you snag a raisin or two.

MAKES 12 BUNS

FOR THE RAISINS

- 1 cup (140 g) raisins
- 1 cup (237 ml) warm water
- 1 teaspoon vanilla extract

FOR THE BUNS

- 3¾ cups (450 g) all-purpose flour
- ¼ cup (50 g) granulated sugar
- 2¼ teaspoons (1 packet) instant yeast (see Note)
- 1 teaspoon salt
- 1 teaspoon ground cinnamon
- 1 cup (237 ml) milk of choice
- 1 large egg
- 1 large egg yolk
- 4 tablespoons (½ stick/57 g) unsalted butter, cubed
- 1 teaspoon vanilla extract
- Vegetable oil, for greasing the bowl

FOR THE GLAZE

- 1 large egg
- 2 tablespoons unsalted butter, melted

FOR SERVING (OPTIONAL)

- Butter
- Jam
- Honey

1 **SOAK THE RAISINS:** Place the raisins into a small bowl and pour over the warm water and the vanilla. Stir to combine, then cover and let rest at room temperature for 30 minutes. Drain the liquid, then set aside.

2 **MAKE THE BUNS:** In a large bowl, combine the flour, sugar, yeast, salt, and cinnamon. Whisk together until blended, then set aside.

3 In a small saucepan, combine the milk, egg, and egg yolk and whisk together until blended. Add the butter. Set the heat to low and stir occasionally until the butter melts and the mixture reaches 110° to 115°F (43° to 46°C) on a digital thermometer. The mixture should feel warm but not hot. Add the vanilla and stir to combine. Pour the liquid mixture into the dry mixture and stir until no dry streaks remain and the dough begins to form. Transfer the dough to a clean, lightly floured work surface and knead by hand for 5 to 6 minutes, until smooth and stretchy. Add the raisins and knead until evenly incorporated into the dough, another 1 to 2 minutes. Lightly grease the mixing bowl with a

recipe continues

few drops of oil and place the dough into the bowl, then cover with a damp kitchen towel and let rise for 60 minutes to 1 hour 30 minutes, until doubled in size.

4 Line a baking sheet with parchment paper and set aside.

5 Transfer the dough to the lightly floured work surface and stretch into a log about 16 inches long. Cut the dough into 12 equal pieces and shape each piece into a smooth ball with the seam at the bottom. Place the rolls on the prepared baking sheet, spacing them evenly. Cover lightly with a damp kitchen towel and let rise for 30 minutes.

6 Preheat the oven to 350°F (177°C).

7 **MAKE THE GLAZE:** In a small bowl, whisk together the egg and 1 tablespoon water until smooth.

8 Brush the tops and sides of the buns lightly with the egg mixture, then bake for about 20 minutes, or until deeply golden. As soon as the buns come out of the oven, brush them lightly with the butter. Let cool on the baking sheet for 5 minutes, then transfer to a wire rack to cool completely. Serve warm or at room temperature, with butter, jam, or honey, if desired. Bone Appetit!

NOTE

This recipe uses instant yeast, which doesn't require proofing and can be added directly to the other ingredients. If substituting active dry yeast, it must be proofed first, using the following method: When heating the milk mixture, add 1 teaspoon sugar. Once the mixture reaches the correct temperature, remove from the heat, add the active dry yeast, and stir to combine. Let rest until the yeast is foamy, about 5 minutes, then proceed with the recipe.

SPOOKY SNACKS AND SIDES

RUNNING FROM MONSTERS ALL NIGHT CAN BUILD UP AN APPETITE.

A simple snack gives you that extra boost of energy to think quicker and scream louder. Preparing a batch of Flaming Hot Popcorn (page 75) sparked by **SCREAM** takes only a few minutes, leaving you plenty of time to refuel . . . and find a working telephone. If you're feeling gutsy, Entrails on Toast (page 47) in honor of **THE ADDAMS FAMILY** or Dead Man's Toes (page 64) unearthed from **HOCUS POCUS** are killer snacks that will murder your hunger. And no horror movie marathon would be complete without Louis's Smoked Salmon Dip from Nova Scotia (page 63), inspired by the classic party scene in **GHOSTBUSTERS**. Whether you're craving something spicy, salty, grilled, or fried, you'll find it here in Spooky Snacks and Sides.

"Welcome, honored guests.
Entrails?"
—MORTICIA ADDAMS

ENTRAILS ON TOAST (WILD MUSHROOM CROSTINI)

THE ADDAMS FAMILY (1991)

The snacks for your next séance are sorted. Conjure the spirit of Uncle Fester, who's been missing in the Bermuda Triangle for twenty-five years. Call forth the candlelight and prepare Grandmama's beloved bites for your summoning. Toasted slices of baguette are topped with melty Gruyère cheese and a magical mushroom pâté made with wild mushrooms, Kalamata olives, fresh parsley, garlic, lemon zest, and red pepper flakes. Garnished with salmon roe jewels, this treasured toast is the perfect snack to eat while contacting the other side.

MAKES ABOUT 20 MINI TOASTS

FOR THE MUSHROOM PÂTÉ

- 2 tablespoons extra-virgin olive oil
- 16 ounces (454 g) mushrooms of choice, coarsely chopped (18 to 22 medium mushrooms)
- 4 large garlic cloves (20 g), finely chopped
- ¼ cup (12 g) fresh Italian parsley, finely chopped
- 1 tablespoon chopped Kalamata olives
- 1¼ teaspoons salt
- ½ teaspoon freshly ground black pepper
- ⅛ teaspoon red pepper flakes
- Grated zest from 1 lemon

FOR ASSEMBLY

- 1 crusty baguette, thinly sliced
- Extra-virgin olive oil, for brushing the bread
- 4 ounces (113 g) Gruyère cheese, thinly sliced
- Salmon roe, for garnish
- Kalamata olives, halved, for garnish

1 **MAKE THE PÂTÉ:** Place a large skillet over medium heat. When the skillet is hot (see Notes, page 27), drizzle in the olive oil. Add the mushrooms and cook for 10 to 12 minutes, until they soften and release their juices. Then add the garlic, parsley, olives, salt, black pepper, red pepper flakes, and lemon zest. Toss to combine, cook for 30 seconds, then remove from the heat. Transfer the mushroom mixture to a food processor and blend until smooth. Let the mixture rest until cool enough to handle, about 15 minutes, then transfer to a piping bag or a large zip-top plastic bag with one corner cut off. Set aside.

2 **ASSEMBLE THE TOASTS:** Preheat the broiler to high. Have a baking sheet near the stove. Place a large skillet over medium heat. Lightly brush both sides of the baguette slices with olive oil, then place the slices in the hot skillet. Cook until golden underneath, then flip the slices and cook until the bottom is golden. Transfer the toasts to the baking sheet, then top each one with a slice of Gruyère cheese. Use the piping bag to pipe swirls of the pâté on top of the cheese.

3 Place the baking sheet under the broiler until the cheese has melted, about 1 minute, making sure to watch the toasts to ensure they don't burn. Garnish each toast with salmon roe and halved Kalamata olives and serve warm. Bone Appetit!

GRILLED PRAWNS WITH A TARRAGON-MUSTARD DIP

BEETLEJUICE
(1988)

Don't you just hate it when you're hosting an important dinner party and the appetizers come alive and attack your guests? Thankfully, that won't happen with this ghost-proof recipe. This celebrated side of lightly grilled prawns, paired with a zesty dip made with Dijon mustard, minced shallots, red and white wine vinegars, fresh parsley, and tarragon, is guaranteed to make your friends get up and dance the calypso.

SERVES 6 TO 8

- ½ cup (118 ml) extra-virgin olive oil
- ¼ cup (59 ml) white wine vinegar
- ¼ cup (59 ml) red wine vinegar
- ¼ cup (65 g) Dijon mustard
- ¼ cup (12 g) finely chopped fresh Italian parsley
- ¼ cup (40 g) finely chopped shallots
- 2 teaspoons salt
- ½ teaspoon freshly ground black pepper
- ½ teaspoon dried tarragon
- ¼ teaspoon red pepper flakes
- 1½ pounds (680 g) raw jumbo prawns, peeled and deveined, tails on (35 to 40 prawns)
- 35 to 40 wooden skewers (4 to 6 inches long)

1. In a medium bowl, whisk together the olive oil, white wine vinegar, red wine vinegar, mustard, parsley, shallots, salt, black pepper, tarragon, and red pepper flakes until blended. Set aside.

2. Place a grill pan or skillet over medium-high heat. Place each shrimp on a skewer lengthwise to prevent it from curling as it cooks. Lay the shrimp skewers on the hot grill pan or skillet and cook for 2 to 3 minutes, then flip and cook for an additional 2 to 3 minutes, until the shrimp looks pink and opaque throughout.

3. To serve, remove the wooden skewers and arrange 5 shrimp in a small bowl with their tails facing upward. Pour a generous amount of sauce in the center of each bowl and serve warm. Bone Appetit!

"This was not a hallucination. This was real. We all experienced a super-powerful paranormal experience, and it was real."

—DELIA DEETZ

"Music is my language and
the world es mi familia."
—MIGUEL RIVERA

MASHED POTATO TAQUITOS

COCO

(2017)

In Miguel's charming hometown of Santa Cecilia, there is music around every corner. During Día de los Muertos, mariachi bands serenade the main plaza, filling the streets with songs while inviting aromas of homemade Mexican food float through the air. These crispy, golden taquitos—also known as flautas or "flutes"—are musically magnificent. Loaded with creamy mashed potatoes and seasoned with scallions and a hint of garlic, they're the perfect snack for your next fiesta.

MAKES 18 TO 20 TAQUITOS

- 1 pound (454 g) russet potatoes (1 to 2 potatoes), peeled and cut into ½-inch cubes
- 2 tablespoons unsalted butter
- 1 scallion, finely chopped
- ¼ teaspoon garlic powder
- 1¼ teaspoons salt
- ½ teaspoon freshly ground black pepper
- 18 to 20 (6-inch) corn tortillas
- Vegetable oil, for frying

FOR GARNISH

- Pico de gallo
- Salsa verde
- Guacamole
- Shredded lettuce
- Crumbled Cotija cheese
- Sliced scallions

1 Place the potatoes in a medium pot and add enough cold water to cover them by at least one inch. Cover the pot, set the heat to medium-high, and bring to a boil. Then reduce the heat to low and simmer for about 10 minutes, or until the potatoes are tender when pierced with a fork. Drain the potatoes into a colander, then return them to the pot. Add the butter, scallion, garlic powder, salt, and pepper and mash until smooth and blended. Set aside.

2 Heat a tortilla in the microwave or in a dry skillet until warm and pliable. Scoop about 2 tablespoons of the mashed potato mixture onto the center of the tortilla, then roll up the tortilla to make a tube about 1½ inches wide. If necessary, use a toothpick to keep the tortilla closed. Repeat with the remaining filling and tortillas.

3 Pour the oil into a large skillet until it is ¼ inch deep. Set over medium heat until the surface of the oil shimmers. To test if the oil is hot, place a small piece of tortilla into the skillet; if it immediately begins to bubble, the oil is ready. Place the taquitos seam side down into the oil and cook for 1 to 3 minutes, then flip and cook an additional 1 to 3 minutes, until golden on both sides. Serve hot with your choice of garnishes. Bone Appetit!

ESQUITES MEXICAN STREET CORN SALAD

The world of *Coco* is a vibrant celebration of color. The Rivera family home is decorated with a rainbow of *papel picado* banners, festive handmade garlands, and the warm glow of orange marigold flowers illuminating the *ofrenda*. Their dinner table is just as lively, featuring traditional Tamales de Rajas con Queso (page 87) and sweet Apple Cider Churros with Dulce de Leche (page 155), alongside bountiful bowls of fresh fruit and golden corn on the cob. Esquites is a classic Mexican street food dish, where corn kernels are grilled, then tossed with toppings like butter, mayo, Cotija cheese, garlic, lime, jalapeño, fresh cilantro, and scallions. It's a quick, crowd-pleasing snack with a kaleidoscope of flavors.

COCO
(2017)

SERVES 8 TO 10

6 ears corn, husk and silk removed
2 tablespoons vegetable oil
1 tablespoon unsalted butter
Grated zest from 1 lime
¼ cup (59 ml) lime juice (2 to 3 limes), plus more as needed
1 tablespoon sour cream
1 tablespoon mayonnaise
1 jalapeño pepper, seeded and diced
½ teaspoon chili powder
2 large garlic cloves (10 g), finely chopped
⅓ cup (24 g) fresh cilantro, finely chopped
2 scallions, finely chopped
1 teaspoon salt, plus more as needed
2 ounces (57 g) Cotija cheese, crumbled

FOR GARNISH (OPTIONAL)

Crumbled Cotija cheese
Lime wedges
Chopped fresh cilantro
Chili powder

1. Use a large knife to cut the kernels off the corn by slicing downward along the sides. Transfer to a bowl and set aside.

2. Place a large skillet over medium heat. When hot (see Notes, page 27), drizzle in the oil. Then add the corn kernels and spread into an even layer. Cook for 8 to 10 minutes, stirring occasionally, until the kernels are softened and some begin to turn golden brown. Transfer to a large heatproof bowl, then add the butter and toss to coat the kernels evenly. Let the mixture cool for 5 minutes, then add the lime zest, lime juice, sour cream, mayonnaise, jalapeño, chili powder, garlic, cilantro, scallions, salt, and cheese and toss to combine. Taste for salt and lime juice and adjust as needed. Serve warm or at room temperature and top with your choice of garnishes, if desired. Bone Appetit!

"I have to sing. I have to play. The music, it's not just in me, it *is* me."

—ERNESTO DE LA CRUZ

GOOD BYE

SLUMBER PARTY ARTICHOKE DIP WITH GRUYÈRE AND SPINACH

THE CRAFT
(1996)

In a dimly lit room illuminated by twinkling candles and surrounded by cozy blankets, Sarah, Nancy, Bonnie, and Rochelle gather at Bonnie's house for a late-night slumber party. The girls spend the evening laughing, experimenting with magic, and bonding over snacks and spells. It's easy to imagine this dreamy dip as their sleepover centerpiece. Baked until golden and bubbly, this spellbinding spread—made with artichoke hearts, spinach, garlic, Parmesan, and Gruyère—will leave you levitating. Blessed be.

SERVES 6 TO 8

- Softened butter, for greasing the baking dish
- 8 ounces (227 g) cream cheese, at room temperature
- ½ cup (113 g) sour cream
- ½ cup (113 g) mayonnaise
- 1 (14-ounce/397 g) can artichoke hearts, drained and quartered
- 10 ounces (284 g) frozen chopped spinach, defrosted and squeezed dry
- 1¼ cups (142 g) grated Parmesan cheese, divided
- ¾ cup (85 g) grated Gruyère cheese, divided
- 2 large garlic cloves (10 g), finely chopped
- ¼ teaspoon salt
- ⅛ teaspoon red pepper flakes

SERVING SUGGESTIONS

- Baguette slices
- Tortilla chips
- Crackers
- Raw vegetables

1. Preheat the oven to 375°F (191°C). Use butter to lightly grease a baking dish approximately 9 inches wide, such as a pie plate, skillet, or square baking dish.

2. In a large bowl, stir the cream cheese until smooth and creamy. Add the sour cream and mayonnaise and stir until combined. Add the artichoke hearts, spinach, 1 cup of the Parmesan, ½ cup of the Gruyère, the garlic, salt, and red pepper flakes. Stir until evenly blended, then spread into an even layer in the prepared baking dish. Sprinkle the remaining ¼ cup of Parmesan and ¼ cup of Gruyère over the top, then bake for 25 to 30 minutes, until golden and bubbly. Let rest for 5 minutes, then serve warm with your choice of baguette slices, tortilla chips, crackers, and/or raw vegetables. Bone Appetit!

"Did you guys ever play that game, Light as a Feather, Stiff as a Board?"

—SARAH BAILEY

MINI GRILLED CHEESE TRIANGLES WITH CHIPOTLE AÏOLI

CORALINE

(2009)

Coraline often feels neglected in the real world. Her parents are too busy to spend time with her, and their cooking stinks. But the Other World is warm and welcoming, and every meal is a dream. From breakfasts such as Other World Waffles with Strawberry Sauce (page 31) to desserts like Black Button Cookies (page 159), the Other Mother lovingly prepares all of Coraline's favorite foods, like these Mini Grilled Cheese Triangles. Golden and crispy, and loaded with melty sharp Cheddar cheese and smoked Gouda, the sandwiches feature a spicy, smoky aïoli with chipotle chiles, adobo sauce, garlic, and lime juice. After one bite, you'll understand why Coraline was tempted to stay in the Other World forever.

MAKES 8 SANDWICHES

FOR THE CHIPOTLE AÏOLI

- 3 tablespoons mayonnaise
- 2 tablespoons canned chipotle chiles in adobo sauce, finely chopped
- 1 tablespoon adobo sauce from the can of chiles
- 1 teaspoon freshly squeezed lime juice
- 1 large garlic clove (5 g), finely chopped

FOR ASSEMBLY

- 2 cups (227 g) grated sharp Cheddar cheese
- 2 cups (227 g) grated smoked Gouda cheese
- 16 slices sandwich bread
- Salted butter

1. **MAKE THE CHIPOTLE AÏOLI:** In a small bowl, combine the mayonnaise, chipotle chiles, adobo sauce, lime juice, and garlic and stir until blended. Set aside.

2. **ASSEMBLE THE SANDWICHES:** In a medium bowl, toss the Cheddar and Gouda until evenly mixed. Set aside.

3. Spread about 2 teaspoons of the aïoli on a slice of bread, then top it with about 2 ounces (about ½ cup) of the cheese mixture, spreading the cheese into an even layer. Place a second slice of bread over the cheese to make a sandwich and spread a layer of butter on top of the bread. Repeat to make additional sandwiches. Any remaining aïoli can be saved and used as a dip when serving.

4. Place a large skillet over medium-low heat. When hot (see Notes, page 27), swirl about ½ tablespoon butter in the skillet, spreading it around the pan as it melts. Place a sandwich, butter side up, in the skillet, then cover the skillet. Cook for 2 to 3 minutes, until the underside is lightly golden brown, then flip the sandwich, cover the skillet, and cook for an additional 2 to 3 minutes, until the underside is golden brown and the cheese inside has melted. Repeat with the remaining sandwiches. Cut into triangles and serve immediately. Bone Appetit!

"You'll be so happy here, Coraline. You'll never have to leave again!"

—THE OTHER MOTHER

"There's an eye in me soup."
—FINIS EVERGLOT

EYEBALL SOUP (ROASTED TOMATO SOUP WITH MOZZARELLA EYEBALLS)

CORPSE BRIDE

(2005)

Skeletons aren't exactly known for their hand-eyeball coordination—or their manners. When the dead return to the land of the living, they brazenly crash the Everglot–Van Dort wedding rehearsal without an invitation. The ghouls terrify the guests, ruin the party, and even manage to drop a loose eyeball in Mr. Everglot's soup bowl. In this eye-catching recipe, Roma tomatoes, onion, carrot, celery, and garlic are roasted in the oven until tender and aromatic, then blended with fresh basil and thyme. Ocularly accented by mozzarella eyeballs with pimento-stuffed green olive pupils, this comforting soup is a sight for sore eyes.

SERVES 6 TO 8

- 3 pounds (1361 g) Roma tomatoes, halved
- 1 large yellow onion (400 g), quartered
- 1 medium carrot (50 g), cut into 1-inch pieces
- 1 large celery rib (40 g), cut into 1-inch pieces
- 1 tablespoon salt
- 2 tablespoons extra-virgin olive oil
- 3 large garlic cloves (15 g), peeled and left whole
- 1 tablespoon tomato paste, plus more for the Eyeballs
- ¼ cup (12 g) fresh basil leaves
- 1 teaspoon fresh thyme leaves
- 4 cups (946 ml) chicken or vegetable broth

FOR THE EYEBALLS

- 16 to 24 mozzarella balls (about 1 inch wide, see Note)
- Pimento-stuffed green olives, sliced into rings

1 Preheat the oven to 400°F (204°C) and line a baking sheet with parchment paper.

2 Place the tomatoes, onion, carrot, and celery on the prepared baking sheet. Sprinkle the salt evenly over the vegetables, then drizzle with the olive oil and toss to coat. Bake for 30 minutes, tossing the vegetables halfway through. Add the garlic and continue baking for 15 minutes, or until the vegetables are softened. Let the vegetables cool for 5 minutes, then transfer to a blender. Add the tomato paste, basil, and thyme and blend until smooth.

3 Pour the puréed vegetables into a large saucepan and add the chicken broth. Cover the pan, bring to a simmer over medium-high heat, then immediately remove from the heat.

4 **MAKE THE EYEBALLS:** Place a small drop of tomato paste onto a mozzarella ball, then place an olive slice on top of the paste so it sticks to the ball. Repeat until there are 1 to 3 eyeballs per serving.

5 Pour the soup into wide, shallow bowls about 1 inch deep. Place the eyeballs in the bowl so the olive pupils are visible and serve warm. Bone Appetit!

NOTE

For the mozzarella, look for balls 1 to 1½ inches wide, often labeled as bocconcini or ciliegine.

SMASH BURGER SLIDERS

Consumed by his obsession with the mysterious new neighbor, Charley is too distracted to spend time with his girlfriend, Amy. Feeling frustrated and fed up with his lack of attention and dismissive behavior, she finally snaps. Grabbing her burger, she forcefully smashes it into Charley's face before storming out of the diner. Inspired by this explosive incident, our smash burger sliders are a guaranteed knockout. Grilled to perfection and topped with melty American cheese, thinly sliced onion, dill pickles, and an irresistible special sauce, these pugilistic patties really pack a punch.

MAKES 8 DOUBLE CHEESEBURGER SLIDERS

FOR THE SPECIAL SAUCE

- ½ cup (113 g) mayonnaise
- ¼ cup (68 g) ketchup
- 1 tablespoon sweet pickle relish
- 1 teaspoon yellow mustard
- ½ teaspoon white wine vinegar
- ½ teaspoon salt
- ¼ teaspoon freshly ground black pepper

FOR THE BURGERS

- 1 pound (454 g) ground beef (80% lean/20% fat)
- Salt
- Freshly ground black pepper
- Salted butter
- 8 slider buns (2 to 3 inches wide), cut in half
- Yellow American cheese slices, cut into quarters
- Thinly sliced yellow onion
- Dill pickle slices

1. **MAKE THE SPECIAL SAUCE:** In a small bowl, combine the mayonnaise, ketchup, relish, mustard, vinegar, salt, and pepper and stir until blended. Set aside.

2. **MAKE THE BURGERS:** Divide the beef into 1-ounce portions, loosely forming the beef into a ball shape without squeezing it too tightly. You should have 16 balls. Sprinkle the tops with a pinch each of salt and pepper. Set aside.

3. Place a large skillet over medium heat. When hot (see Notes, page 27), swirl in about ½ tablespoon butter, spreading it around the skillet as it melts. Working in batches, place the slider buns into the skillet cut side down and cook until the undersides are golden and toasted. Set aside.

4. Working in batches, place a few portions of beef into the skillet with the salt and pepper side down, leaving at least 4 inches of space between each one. Sprinkle the tops with a pinch each of salt and pepper, then place a small square of parchment over each portion and use a wide spatula to flatten it until ¼ to ⅛ inch thick. Remove the parchment and cook for 1 to 1½ minutes, until the color begins to change and they look juicy on top. Then flip the patties—if they stick, use the spatula to scrape them off the skillet. Place a small square of cheese onto each patty, then sprinkle some sliced onion on top. Cook for 1 minute, then stack 2 patties on a toasted bun bottom. Repeat with the remaining beef and buns.

5. Garnish with a few pickle slices, then spread the top bun with a generous layer of the special sauce and place it on top to make a sandwich. Bone Appetit!

"I've got a vampire living next door and he's going to kill me if I don't protect myself."

—CHARLEY BREWSTER

LOUIS'S SMOKED SALMON DIP FROM NOVA SCOTIA

Louis Tully knows how to throw a party. He plays the best disco records, his snack game is next level, and best of all, he's able to write off the expenses on his taxes. Sure, his guests may have to deal with an occasional demon dog, but his legendary smoked salmon dip more than makes up for any inconvenience. Simply made with cream cheese, smoked salmon, lemon juice, capers, fresh dill, and chives, this delightful dip is quick, easy, and Keymaster-approved.

SERVES 8 TO 10

- 8 ounces (227 g) cream cheese, at room temperature
- 2 tablespoons heavy cream or half-and-half
- 6 ounces (170 g) smoked salmon
- 2 tablespoons chopped fresh dill, plus more for garnish (optional)
- 2 tablespoons chopped fresh chives, plus more for garnish (optional)
- 1½ tablespoons freshly squeezed lemon juice
- 1 teaspoon capers
- ¼ teaspoon salt
- ¼ teaspoon freshly ground black pepper

SERVING SUGGESTIONS

- Crackers
- Baguette slices
- Raw vegetables

In a food processor, blend the cream cheese until fluffy. Add the heavy cream and blend until smooth. Add the smoked salmon, dill, chives, lemon juice, capers, salt, and pepper and pulse until evenly combined, but not fully puréed. Transfer to a bowl and garnish with more dill and chives, if desired. Serve with crackers, baguette slices, and/or raw veggies. Bone Appetit!

"Hey, this is real smoked salmon from Nova Scotia, Canada, $24.95 a pound. It only cost me $14.12 after tax, though. I'm giving this whole thing as a promotional expense. That's why I invited clients instead of friends."

—LOUIS TULLY

DEAD MAN'S TOES (PIGS IN A BLANKET)

HOCUS POCUS
(1993)

When you're a witch, it's vital to keep a well-stocked pantry. From oil of boil to green newt saliva, potion-making requires a collection of obscure ingredients not typically available at your local grocery store. The key component in the Sanderson Sisters' life-force spell is a dead man's toe, but thankfully you won't need to visit the local morgue to obtain one. These illusory snacks may look like severed appendages, but rest assured—they're far more delicious than they appear.

MAKES 16 TOES

FOR THE DIJON DIP

- **3 tablespoons coarse ground mustard**
- **2 tablespoons Dijon mustard**
- **1 teaspoon mayonnaise**
- **1 large garlic clove (5 g), finely chopped**
- **½ teaspoon white wine vinegar**
- **⅛ teaspoon salt**
- **⅛ teaspoon freshly ground black pepper**

FOR THE TOES

- **1 package refrigerated crescent dough**
- **1 package hot dogs**
- **Ketchup**
- **1 large egg**
- **Sliced almonds**

1. Preheat the oven to 375°F (191°C) and line a baking sheet with parchment paper.

2. **MAKE THE DIJON DIP:** In a small bowl, combine the coarse ground mustard, Dijon mustard, mayonnaise, garlic, vinegar, salt, and pepper and stir until blended. Set aside.

3. **MAKE THE TOES:** Open the package of crescent dough, unroll the dough, and lay it flat on a cutting board. Cut the rectangle of dough into strips about ½ inch wide.

4. Cut the hot dogs in half. To create the toe illusion, first cut a small slice off the round end of the hot dog at an angle, which will make space for the toenail. Using 1 to 2 strips of dough, wrap the flat end of the hot dog to look like a bandage, leaving the round end uncovered. Place on the prepared baking sheet with the toenail facing up. Repeat with the remaining hot dogs and dough. Place a small drop of ketchup (less than ⅛ teaspoon) in the center of each toenail.

5. In a small bowl, stir together the egg with 1 teaspoon water until smooth and blended. Lightly brush the egg wash over the dough strips. Bake for 10 minutes, then remove the baking sheet from the oven and place a sliced almond on each hot dog to create the toenail, using the ketchup as glue. Return to the oven and bake for 3 to 5 minutes, until the dough is golden. Let cool for 5 minutes, then serve warm with the Dijon dip. Bone Appetit!

"Mix blood of owl with the herb that's red. Turn three times, pluck a hair from my head. Add a dash of pox and a dead man's toe."
—WINIFRED SANDERSON

"Dear Great Pumpkin,
I'm looking forward
to your arrival on
Halloween night.
I hope you bring me
lots of presents."
—LINUS

GREAT PUMPKIN SOUP

When the Great Pumpkin rises out of the pumpkin patch, take that as a sign to make a batch of Great Pumpkin Soup. Cozier than Linus's blanket, this warm fall dish is made with deeply roasted and caramelized pumpkin, fresh sage leaves, sauteéed carrots, and a serrano pepper for a hint of heat. Garnished with a swirl of Greek yogurt and a squeeze of lime, this autumnal soup is infinitely tastier than a bagful of rocks.

IT'S THE GREAT PUMPKIN, CHARLIE BROWN (1966)

SERVES 6 TO 8

- 1 medium orange pumpkin (3 to 3½ pounds/1.3 to 1.6 kg)
- 4 tablespoons extra-virgin olive oil, divided
- 1 large yellow onion (400 g), chopped
- 3 large celery ribs (160 g), chopped
- 3 medium carrots (150 g), chopped
- ¼ green apple (65 g), peeled and grated
- 4 large garlic cloves (20 g), finely chopped
- 1 serrano pepper, seeded and chopped
- 4 large fresh sage leaves, finely chopped
- 1 teaspoon salt
- ½ teaspoon ground nutmeg
- ¼ teaspoon ground cinnamon
- 6 cups (1.4 L) chicken or vegetable broth

FOR GARNISH (OPTIONAL)

- Pepitas
- Chopped fresh cilantro
- Plain Greek yogurt or heavy whipping cream
- Lime wedges

1. Preheat the oven to 425°F (218°C) and line a baking sheet with parchment paper.

2. Using a large knife, cut the pumpkin in half, remove the stem, and scoop out all the seeds and pulp. Cut the pumpkin into large pieces, then cut off the skin. Dice the pumpkin into ½-inch cubes and arrange them on the prepared baking sheet. Drizzle with 2 tablespoons of the olive oil and toss to coat evenly. Bake for 35 to 40 minutes, until tender when pierced with a fork, tossing halfway through to ensure they cook evenly.

3. Place a large pot over medium heat and drizzle in the remaining 2 tablespoons of olive oil. When the oil starts to shimmer, add the onion, celery, and carrots and cook for 7 to 10 minutes, until softened. Add the apple, garlic, serrano, sage, salt, nutmeg, and cinnamon and cook for 1 minute. Add the roasted pumpkin and chicken broth, stir to combine, then cover the pot. Increase the heat to medium-high and bring to a boil, stirring occasionally. Once boiling, reduce the heat to low and simmer, covered, for 15 minutes, stirring occasionally. Purée the soup using an immersion blender or by transferring the soup to a standard blender in batches. (Caution: When blending hot liquids, fill the blender only halfway and blend on a slow setting to prevent splatters and burns.)

4. Serve in bowls topped with pepitas, cilantro, a swirl of yogurt, and lime wedges, if desired. Bone Appetit!

SALLY'S SNEAKY ROASTED CAULIFLOWER SOUP WITH FROG'S BREATH AND WORM'S WART

THE NIGHTMARE BEFORE CHRISTMAS (1993)

Like any young ghoul, Sally longs for independence. Her overbearing creator, Dr. Finkelstein, never lets her leave the laboratory, forcing her to resort to nefarious means to escape. After spiking his soup with deadly nightshade, she masks its telltale toxic flavor with aromatic frog's breath and worm's wart. In this poison-free version, oven-roasted cauliflower is brewed with sautéed onion, celery, fresh rosemary, and plenty of frog's breath (aka garlic). Puréed until creamy and topped with a spoonful of worm's wart (capers), this surreptitious soup is just what the doctor ordered.

SERVES 6 TO 8

- **1 large head cauliflower (about 2 pounds/907 g), cut into 2-inch pieces**
- **4 tablespoons extra-virgin olive oil, divided**
- **1 large yellow onion (400 g), chopped**
- **1 large celery rib (40 g), chopped**
- **4 large garlic cloves (20 g), finely chopped**
- **2 teaspoons salt**
- **1 teaspoon minced fresh rosemary**
- **½ teaspoon freshly ground black pepper**
- **4 cups (946 ml) chicken or vegetable broth**
- **Capers, for garnish**

1 Preheat the oven to 425°F (218°C) and line a baking sheet with parchment paper. Place the cauliflower on the sheet, then drizzle with 2 tablespoons of the olive oil and toss to coat. Spread the cauliflower in an even layer, then bake for 20 to 30 minutes, until tender when pierced with a fork. Set aside.

2 Place a large saucepan over medium heat. When hot (see Notes, page 27), swirl in the remaining 2 tablespoons of olive oil. Add the onion and celery and cook for 8 to 10 minutes, until softened. Add the garlic, salt, rosemary, and pepper and cook for 1 minute. Add the chicken broth and the roasted cauliflower and stir to combine. Cover the pan, increase the heat to medium-high, and bring to a boil. Once boiling, reduce the heat to low and simmer for 15 minutes, stirring occasionally. Purée the soup using an immersion blender or by transferring the soup to a standard blender in batches. (Caution: When blending hot liquids, fill the blender only halfway and blend on a slow setting to prevent splatters and burns.) Serve warm, garnished with capers. Bone Appetit!

"Worm's wart! Mmm! . . . and . . . frog's breath?"

—DR. FINKELSTEIN

"So, come up to the lab and
see what's on the slab.
I see you shiver
with antici . . . pation."
—DR. FRANK-N-FURTER

DR. FRANK-N-FURTER'S MINI FRANKFURTERS

THE ROCKY HORROR PICTURE SHOW
(1975)

On that dark and stormy night when Brad and Janet arrive at the castle seeking help with a flat tire, they unexpectedly become guests at a party that will change their lives forever. Dazzled by drinks, drugs, and debauched dancers doing the Time Warp, the young couple feel uneasy at first, but quickly join in all the fun, encouraged by their enigmatic Transylvanian host, Dr. Frank-N-Furter. Inspired by his fiery personality, these spicy skewers are a double feature of flavor. Smoked sausages and chewy rice cakes are grilled to perfection then brushed with a sweet and spicy gochujang sauce. Finished with a sprinkle of toasted sesame seeds, this may just be Dr. Frank-N-Furter's greatest creation yet.

MAKES 16 SKEWERS

FOR THE SAUCE

- ¼ cup (60 g) gochujang (see Note)
- 2 tablespoons ketchup
- 2 tablespoons light corn syrup
- 2 tablespoons soy sauce
- 4 large garlic cloves (20 g), finely chopped

FOR ASSEMBLY

- 32 tube-shaped tteokbokki-tteok (Korean rice cakes, see Note)
- 16 wooden skewers (4 to 6 inches long)
- 32 smoked cocktail sausages
- Toasted sesame seeds, for garnish

1 **MAKE THE SAUCE:** In a small bowl, combine the gochujang, ketchup, corn syrup, soy sauce, 2 tablespoons water, and the garlic and stir until blended. Set aside.

2 **ASSEMBLE THE SKEWERS:** First, soften the rice cakes according to package directions—typically by boiling them in water, then draining and rinsing with cold water.

3 Assemble each skewer with two rice cakes and two sausages, alternating between the two.

4 Place a skillet or grill pan over medium heat. When hot (see Notes, page 27), lay the skewers in the skillet and cook for 1 to 3 minutes until the undersides are golden and crisp, then flip and cook an additional 1 to 3 minutes. Remove the skewers from the skillet, brush them generously with the sauce, and sprinkle with sesame seeds. Serve warm, with additional sauce for dipping. Bone Appetit!

NOTE

Gochujang and rice cakes are common ingredients in Korean cuisine. Gochujang is a spicy-sweet, fermented paste, and tteokbokki-tteok are thick and chewy, tube-shaped rice cakes. Both are available in Asian markets and online.

HOT POTATO, BLESS MY SOUL PATATAS BRAVAS WITH A (TIM) CURRY AÏOLI

THE ROCKY HORROR PICTURE SHOW (1975)

Poor Eddie can't catch a break. First, Dr. Frank-N-Furter uses him as a partial brain donor, then locks him in a freezer, murders him with a pickaxe, and serves him as an entrée to his unsuspecting dinner guests. At least Eddie gets to light up the screen in a showstopping musical number before his untimely demise—complete with sparkling backup dancers, a grand, wall-crashing motorcycle entrance, and an electrifying saxophone solo. In honor of his song, "Hot Patootie," this appetizer is a spirited spin on patatas bravas, a classic Spanish tapas dish. Featuring crispy, golden roasted potatoes drizzled with a zesty (Tim) Curry aïoli, this spicy side will soon become a cult classic.

SERVES 5 TO 6

FOR THE (TIM) CURRY AÏOLI

½ cup (113 g) mayonnaise
1 tablespoon curry powder
1 teaspoon ground cayenne pepper
1 teaspoon fresh lemon juice
½ teaspoon honey
½ teaspoon ground turmeric
¼ teaspoon smoked paprika
¼ teaspoon garlic powder
¼ teaspoon salt

FOR THE POTATOES

2 pounds (907 g) russet potatoes (2 to 4 medium potatoes), cut into 1-inch pieces
1½ teaspoons salt, divided
3 tablespoons extra-virgin olive oil
½ teaspoon ground cumin
Chopped fresh parsley, for garnish

1 Preheat the oven to 500°F (260°C) and line a baking sheet with parchment paper.

2 **MAKE THE AÏOLI:** In a small bowl, combine the mayonnaise, curry powder, cayenne pepper, lemon juice, honey, turmeric, paprika, garlic powder, and salt. Stir until blended, then set aside.

3 **MAKE THE POTATOES:** Place the potatoes into a large saucepan and add enough cold water to cover them by at least 1 inch. Add 1 teaspoon of the salt, then cover the pan and bring to a boil over medium-high heat. Once boiling, reduce the heat to low and simmer for 5 minutes. Drain the potatoes, then return them to the pan. Add the remaining ½ teaspoon of salt, the olive oil, and cumin and toss gently to coat, being careful not to break up the potatoes. Transfer to the prepared baking sheet and spread the potatoes in an even layer. Bake for 30 to 35 minutes, until golden and crispy, tossing halfway through to ensure they cook evenly. Transfer to a serving dish and top with a generous drizzle of the aïoli and a sprinkle of parsley. Serve hot, with additional aïoli for dipping. Bone Appetit!

“Hot patootie, bless my soul,
I really love that rock ’n’ roll.”

—EDDIE

FLAMING HOT POPCORN

SCREAM

(1996)

Casey Becker is looking forward to a quiet evening at home. With her parents out on a dinner date, she has the house to herself. She picks out a scary movie and sets a pan of popcorn on the stove, but everything takes a terrifying turn after answering a call from a deranged murderer. As the menacing voice threatens her life and reveals he's outside, she forgets all about the popcorn—leaving it to go up in flames. This fiery popcorn pays tribute to Casey and one of horror's most iconic opening scenes. Put on a spooky flick and get ready for an intensely flavored treat that tastes like everyone's favorite *Flamin' Hot* snacks. Just don't answer the phone before the movie starts.

SERVES 3 TO 4

- 2 tablespoons Cheddar cheese powder (see Note)
- 2 teaspoons ground cayenne pepper
- 1 teaspoon salt
- ¾ teaspoon monosodium glutamate (see Note)
- ¾ teaspoon citric acid (see Note)
- ½ teaspoon freshly ground black pepper
- ½ teaspoon garlic powder
- ½ teaspoon sugar
- ¼ teaspoon onion powder
- 1 package microwave popcorn of choice

1 In a small bowl, combine the Cheddar cheese powder, cayenne pepper, salt, monosodium glutamate, citric acid, black pepper, garlic powder, sugar, and onion powder and stir until evenly blended. Set aside.

2 Prepare the bag of popcorn according to the package directions. Transfer the popcorn to a large serving bowl, then slowly add the cheese mixture, tossing the popcorn as you add the powder to coat it evenly. Bone Appetit!

NOTE

Cheddar cheese powder, monosodium glutamate, and citric acid can all be found online or in cooking supply stores. Citric acid is powdered lemon juice, while monosodium glutamate is a naturally occurring salt found in foods like tomatoes, cheese, and mushrooms.

"Do you like scary movies?"

—GHOSTFACE

CUCUMBER SANDWICHES WITH BUTTER, NOT MARGARINE

THE WITCHES
(1990)

Bruno Jenkins is a greedy boy. Before being lured into the Grand High Witch's trap with the promise of six whole bars of cream-whip hazelnut milk chocolate, he spends the day gorging himself on Bewitching Raisin Buns (page 39) and tea cakes in the hotel dining room. He has strong opinions when it comes to food, insisting to Luke that the best cucumber sandwiches are prepared with butter, not margarine. Afternoon tea wouldn't be the same without these delicate British treats. Made with layers of crisp cucumber slices and a tangy herbed cream cheese spread featuring fresh dill, chives, mint, and a splash of lemon juice, these bite-size snacks are completely margarine-free—with Bruno Jenkins's seal of approval.

MAKES 8 FULL-SIZE SANDWICHES OR 16 FINGER SANDWICHES

- 1 large cucumber
- 1 teaspoon salt, divided
- 8 ounces (227 g) cream cheese, at room temperature
- 2 tablespoons mayonnaise
- 1 tablespoon chopped fresh dill
- 1 tablespoon chopped fresh chives
- 2 teaspoons chopped fresh mint leaves
- 2 teaspoons freshly squeezed lemon juice
- ¼ teaspoon freshly ground black pepper
- 16 slices white sandwich bread
- Salted butter (not margarine), at room temperature

1. Using a sharp knife or mandoline, cut the cucumber into very thin slices, about ⅛ inch. Place the slices into a colander and toss with ½ teaspoon of the salt until evenly coated. Let drain for 30 minutes, then pat the slices dry and set aside.

2. In a medium bowl, combine the cream cheese, mayonnaise, dill, chives, mint, lemon juice, pepper, and the remaining ½ teaspoon of salt. Stir until blended and set aside.

3. Spread about 2 tablespoons of the cream cheese mixture onto a slice of bread, then arrange about 9 slices of cucumber over the top, overlapping them in an even layer. Spread a generous layer of butter (not margarine) onto another slice of bread and place it on top of the cucumber to create a sandwich. Repeat with the remaining bread, cheese mixture, cucumber, and butter. Use a large, serrated knife to remove the crusts, then cut the sandwich into triangles or rectangles. Bone Appetit!

"I hope there's butter in the sandwiches today. I really do hate margarine."

—BRUNO JENKINS

"I don't want cock-a-leekie. I don't like cock-a-leekie. I like cress. So just take that back to the kitchen and tell the chef de cuisine that there's one more order for cress soup. Now, there's a laddie."
—MR. JENKINS

HOTEL EXCELSIOR'S CREAMY CRESS SOUP

THE WITCHES
(1990)

The cress soup at the Hotel Excelsior is world-famous. During dinner, when Mr. Jenkins notices a group of women enjoying bowls of this vibrant, emerald-green soup—while he's stuck with a boring cup of cock-a-leekie—he demands to be included. Little does he know, the cress soup is poisoned with Formula 86, a magic potion that transforms people into mice. Rest assured, there is no danger of transmogrification with this recipe. In our potion-free version, peppery watercress is simmered with creamy potatoes, sautéed shallots, and fresh thyme. Blended until smooth and garnished with a drizzle of cream, this satisfying soup will leave you spellbound—Formula 86 not included.

SERVES 6 TO 8

- 2 tablespoons unsalted butter
- 2 cups (260 g) chopped shallots (4 to 6 shallots)
- ¼ cup (59 ml) dry white wine, such as Sauvignon Blanc or Pinot Grigio
- 1 pound (454 g) russet potatoes (1 to 2 potatoes), peeled and cut into 1-inch cubes
- 1 sprig fresh thyme, leaves removed, stem discarded
- 1 teaspoon salt
- 4 cups (946 ml) chicken or vegetable broth
- 8 ounces (227 g) watercress (about 6 bunches), plus more for garnish
- Heavy cream, for garnish

Place a large saucepan over medium heat. When hot (see Notes, page 27), melt the butter. Once the butter melts, add the shallots and cook for about 5 minutes, or until softened. Add the wine and stir to deglaze the pan. Then add the potatoes, thyme, salt, and chicken broth. Cover the pan, bring to a simmer, then reduce the heat and cook for about 10 minutes, or until the potatoes are tender when pierced with a fork. Turn off the heat, then add the watercress and stir until wilted. Purée the soup using an immersion blender or by transferring the soup to a standard blender in batches. (Caution: When blending hot liquids, fill the blender only halfway and blend on a slow setting to prevent splatters and burns.) Serve warm, and garnish with a few watercress leaves and a drizzle of cream. Bone Appetit!

MONSTROUS MAINS

A FULL MOON LOOMS OVER THE HORIZON AS A CHILLING BREEZE RUSTLES DRIED LEAVES ACROSS THE GROUND.

Somewhere in the distance, the howl of a lone werewolf pierces the night. AWOOOOO! It's dinner time! This chapter includes nine unnerving entrées to sink your fangs into. Craving insects? Deceiving Chinese Takeout Noodles with Shiitake Mushroom Worms (page 101) inspired by THE LOST BOYS are a great source of protein. Suspect your new neighbor is a vampire? Charley's Garlicky Pasta Puttanesca (page 93) in homage to FRIGHT NIGHT will keep you safe. Want to dine in style like the Addams Family? Grandmama's Spécialité de la Maison (page 84) is a jet-black squid ink paella that's drop-dead delicious. Light some candles, put on a spooky playlist, and let the creepy cooking commence!

GRANDMAMA'S SPÉCIALITÉ DE LA MAISON (SQUID INK PAELLA)

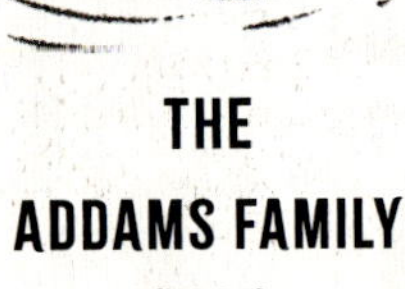

THE ADDAMS FAMILY (1991)

Grandmama is the heart of the Addams family. She prepares all the meals, from appetizers like Entrails on Toast (page 47), to breakfasts of squirming purple oatmeal. To commemorate Fester's return from the Bermuda Triangle, she whips up her "Spécialité de la Maison," complete with tentacles and glistening eyeballs. This classic Spanish dish features fresh shrimp, prawns, mussels, and calamari served over tomato-saffron rice tinted jet-black with squid ink. Garnished with parsley and a squeeze of lemon, this onyx entrée is a seafood celebration.

SERVES 4

- ¼ cup (59 ml) extra-virgin olive oil
- 2 to 4 jumbo prawns, head-on
- 4 to 6 large shrimp, peeled and deveined
- 2 squid, sliced into rings, tentacles kept whole
- 1 medium yellow onion (350 g), chopped
- 2 medium Roma tomatoes (245 g), chopped
- 8 large garlic cloves (40 g), finely chopped
- 1½ teaspoons salt
- ½ teaspoon smoked paprika
- 1½ cups (287 g) short-grain rice, such as Bomba, Arborio, or Calrose
- 3 cups (710 ml) fish broth or chicken broth, plus more as needed
- 1 tablespoon squid ink
- ½ teaspoon saffron threads
- 4 to 6 mussels
- Chopped fresh Italian parsley, for garnish
- Lemon wedges

1. Place a 12-inch paella pan or skillet over medium heat and pour in the olive oil. When the oil starts to shimmer, place the prawns and shrimp into the pan and cook for 1 to 2 minutes per side, until pink and opaque throughout. Transfer the prawns and shrimp to a plate and set aside. Place the squid—rings and tentacles—into the oil and cook for 1 minute, stirring occasionally. Transfer the squid to a plate and set aside, keeping the flame on medium heat.

2. Add the onion to the pan and cook for 5 to 7 minutes, until softened. Add the tomatoes, garlic, salt, and paprika and cook for 4 to 5 minutes. Add the rice and toss to combine. Add the fish broth and squid ink, then use your fingers to crush and sprinkle the saffron into the pan. Stir until blended, then spread the mixture into an even, smooth layer. Bring to a boil, then reduce the heat to medium-low and simmer for 20 minutes without stirring. If too much liquid evaporates, add a few tablespoons of fish broth, as needed. If it boils too vigorously, reduce the heat to a simmer.

3. At the 20-minute mark, taste the rice—it should be slightly undercooked and al dente. If it is too crunchy, continue cooking and add more fish broth as needed. Arrange the mussels and prepared squid on top of the paella, and continue cooking without stirring for 5 minutes. Arrange the prawns and shrimp on top of the paella, turn off the heat, cover the pan, and let rest for 5 minutes. Garnish with parsley and serve (see Note) with lemon wedges. Bone Appetit!

NOTE

When serving the paella, be sure to scrape the crispy bits of rice from the bottom of the pan. They're the best part!

"Start with the eyes."

—GRANDMAMA ADDAMS

TAMALES DE RAJAS CON QUESO

Every dinner is a special occasion at the Rivera house. Miguel lives with his extended family, and each meal feels like a fiesta filled with laughter, engaging conversations, and the best Mexican food you've ever tasted. Stacks of crispy Mashed Potato Taquitos (page 51) and colorful bowls of Esquites Mexican Street Corn Salad (page 52) decorate the dining room table, with homemade tamales taking center stage. In this classic recipe, poblano peppers are roasted and blackened over fire, then cut into thin strips (*rajas*), layered with Monterey Jack cheese, and nestled in soft masa dough. Wrapped in corn husks and steamed until tender, each golden tamale is a tiny treasure, waiting to be opened.

COCO
(2017)

MAKES 12 TO 16 TAMALES

16 dried corn husks (see Note)
3 to 4 large mild green peppers, such as poblano or Anaheim
2½ cups (300 g) masa harina
1½ teaspoons salt
1 teaspoon baking powder
¾ cup (177 ml) vegetable oil
2 cups (473 ml) chicken or vegetable broth
12 ounces (340 g) Monterey Jack cheese, cut into ¼-inch-thick matchsticks
Salsa verde, for serving (optional)

1 Place the corn husks into a large bowl of water, then place a second bowl on top of the husks to keep them submerged. Soak for 1 hour.

2 Meanwhile, roast the peppers using a gas stove or an oven. If using a gas stove, place the whole peppers directly on the flame for 3 to 4 minutes, using tongs to turn them occasionally until the skins are evenly blackened and blistered. If using an oven, halve the peppers, place them cut side down on a baking sheet, and roast at 450°F (232°C) for 30 to 40 minutes. Whichever method you use—as soon as the peppers have finished cooking, place them into a heatproof bowl and cover tightly with plastic wrap. Let the peppers rest for 15 to 20 minutes to loosen the skin. Once they're cool enough to handle, peel the skins off, remove the stems and seeds, and cut the peppers into thin slices. Set aside.

3 To make the dough, combine the masa harina, salt, and baking powder in a large bowl. Add the oil and stir to combine. Add the chicken broth and stir until smooth and blended.

4 To assemble the tamales, first remove a corn husk from the water and pat it dry. Place the husk glossy side up on the counter with the narrow end pointed toward you. Place about 3 tablespoons of the dough near the wide end

recipe continues

"We made all this food, set out the things they loved in life, mijo. All this work to bring the family together."

—ABUELITA

of the husk, and spread it into a 4-inch square, leaving about ½ inch of space between the dough and the top of the husk. Lay a few strips of roasted peppers and matchsticks of cheese down the center of the square of dough. Fold the right side of the husk over the filling, then fold the left side over like a brochure, gently pressing the tamale together. Fold up the excess husk at the bottom, then set the tamale on a plate, ensuring that it stays closed. Repeat with the remaining husks, dough, and filling.

5 Place a steamer basket into a large pot and fill with water until the level is just below the steamer basket. Vertically arrange the tamales open side up in the pot, resting against one another so they remain standing. Cover the pot, bring to a boil, then reduce the heat and simmer for 1 hour, checking the water level occasionally and adding more water if needed, so the pot does not dry out. Turn off the heat, uncover the pot, and let the tamales rest for 20 minutes. Serve warm, with salsa verde. Bone Appetit!

NOTE

Dried corn husks are available in the Latin section of many grocery stores.

SPAGHETTI AND MEATBALLS WITH EXTRA GARLIC

Sam and his friends, Edgar and Alan, also known as the Frog Brothers, suspect that his mom's boyfriend, Max, is secretly a vampire. They test his weaknesses during a date-night dinner by purposely spilling holy water into his lap, shoving mirrors in front of his face, and replacing a dish of grated Parmesan cheese with chopped raw garlic. However, since he was invited in as a guest, he's immune to their screening, making the tests inconclusive. The next time you need to examine a suspected vampire—or if you're simply craving pasta and meatballs with the robust flavors of tomatoes and extra garlic—this scrutinizing supper will certainly suss the situation.

THE LOST BOYS
(1987)

SERVES 4 TO 6

FOR THE MEATBALLS

- ½ cup (38 g) panko breadcrumbs
- ¼ cup (59 ml) whole milk
- 1 large egg
- ¼ cup (28 g) Parmesan cheese, grated
- 2 large garlic cloves (10 g), finely chopped
- ½ small yellow onion (about 140 g), grated
- 2 tablespoons (6 g) chopped fresh parsley
- 1 teaspoon salt
- ½ teaspoon freshly ground black pepper
- ¼ teaspoon dried oregano
- ¼ teaspoon dried thyme
- ¼ teaspoon red pepper flakes
- 8 ounces (227 g) ground beef (80% lean/20% fat)
- 8 ounces (227 g) ground pork

FOR THE PASTA

- 1 (28-ounce/794 g) can whole peeled Italian tomatoes
- 1¼ teaspoons salt, plus more for the pasta water
- 2 tablespoons extra-virgin olive oil
- 5 large garlic cloves (25 g), finely chopped
- ¼ cup (60 ml) dry red wine, such as Pinot Noir, Merlot, or Chianti
- 1 tablespoon unsalted butter
- 1 sprig fresh rosemary
- ½ teaspoon sugar
- ⅛ teaspoon red pepper flakes
- 1 pound (454 g) dried spaghetti
- Parmesan cheese, for garnish (optional)

1 Preheat the oven to 450°F (232°C) and line a baking sheet with parchment paper.

2 **MAKE THE MEATBALLS:** In a medium bowl, combine the breadcrumbs and milk, tossing to coat the breadcrumbs evenly. Let the mixture rest for 5 to 10 minutes. Then add the egg, Parmesan, garlic, onion, parsley, salt, black pepper, oregano, thyme, and red pepper flakes. Stir until blended, then set aside.

3 In a large bowl, combine the beef and pork, using your hands to blend the two meats together. Add the breadcrumb mixture, then continue using your hands to combine until evenly blended—avoid overmixing, as this can result in meatballs that are too dense and tough. Form the mixture into 1½-inch balls, about 45 grams each, then place them on the prepared baking sheet.

recipe continues

This will make approximately 16 meatballs. Bake for about 15 minutes, or until golden brown.

4 **MAKE THE PASTA:** Pour the entire can of tomatoes, including the liquid, into a medium bowl. Using your hands, squeeze and crush the tomatoes until they form a chunky purée. Set aside.

5 Fill a large pot with salted water (about 1 teaspoon salt per quart of water) and bring to a boil over high heat.

6 While the water is heating, place a large skillet over medium heat and swirl in the olive oil. When the oil starts to shimmer, add the garlic and cook for 30 seconds. Add the tomatoes, wine, butter, rosemary, the 1¼ teaspoons salt, the sugar, and red pepper flakes and stir to combine. Bring to a simmer and cook for 15 minutes uncovered, stirring occasionally. Then add the cooked meatballs, toss gently, and simmer for 5 minutes.

7 While the sauce is simmering, cook the pasta. By now, the water should be boiling. Cook the spaghetti according to package directions until al dente. Drain the spaghetti, then toss it with the tomato sauce and meatballs—either in the skillet or the pot. Serve with Parmesan for garnish, if desired. Bone Appetit!

NOTE

The uncooked meatballs freeze well and can be saved for future use: After forming the meatballs, place them on a baking sheet, cover, and place in the freezer for about 4 hours, or until frozen. Then, transfer the frozen meatballs to a zip-top bag or sealed container and store for up to 2 months. When ready to use, place the frozen meatballs on a baking sheet and bake for 20 minutes at 350°F (177°C).

"We've been aware of some very serious vampire activity in this town for a long time."
—EDGAR FROG

"Get some garlic—links of the stuff you can wear around your neck and hang from your window."
—EVIL ED

CHARLEY'S GARLICKY PASTA PUTTANESCA

Charley Brewster is convinced that his next-door neighbor, Jerry Dandridge, is a murderous vampire, but no one believes him, not even the police. Fearing he might be the next victim, he frantically nails his bedroom windows shut and hangs crucifixes and garlands of garlic in a desperate attempt to repel the fiend. This sanctifying spaghetti, made with Italian tomatoes, fresh parsley, Kalamata olives, capers—and extra garlic—is fragrant, delectable, and sure to keep all the vampires away.

SERVES 4

- 2 (28-ounce/794 g) cans whole peeled Italian tomatoes
- 1 teaspoon salt, plus more for the pasta water
- 1 pound (454 g) dried spaghetti
- ¼ cup (59 ml) extra-virgin olive oil
- ½ cup (82 g) Kalamata olives, halved
- ½ cup (24 g) fresh Italian parsley, chopped, plus more for garnish (optional)
- ¼ cup (45 g) capers, drained
- 5 large garlic cloves (25 g), finely chopped
- 8 anchovy filets from a can, finely chopped
- 1 teaspoon dried oregano
- ⅛ teaspoon red pepper flakes

1. Open the cans of tomatoes, then remove the tomatoes one at a time, gently squeezing them with your hand to remove as much liquid as possible—it's best to do this over the sink, as it can be messy. Place the squeezed tomatoes into a bowl and set aside. Discard the remaining liquid or save for another use.

2. Fill a large pot with salted water (about 1 teaspoon salt per quart of water) and bring to a boil over high heat. Add the spaghetti and cook according to package directions until al dente.

3. Meanwhile, combine the squeezed tomatoes and the olive oil in a large, deep skillet. Set the skillet over medium heat and bring to a simmer, stirring occasionally. Once simmering, add the olives, parsley, capers, garlic, anchovies, the 1 teaspoon of salt, the oregano, and red pepper flakes and stir to combine.

4. Once the pasta is done cooking, reserve about 1 cup of the pasta water, then drain the spaghetti and transfer it to the skillet. Toss to combine, and add a few tablespoons of the reserved pasta water if it appears dry. Garnish with parsley, if desired, and serve hot. Bone Appetit!

CRISPY BAKED SCROD WITH LEMON AND PARMESAN

HOCUS POCUS
(1993)

The Sanderson Sisters—Winnie, Sarah, and Mary—are a trio of evil witches on the hunt for children. Winnie, the eldest and most powerful, leads the group, while Sarah uses her enchanting singing voice to lure kids to their doom, and Mary has a superhuman sense of smell, allowing her to detect them from afar. On Halloween night, they scour the streets of downtown Salem in pursuit of Max and Dani, but Mary's nose misleads them to an alley behind a seafood restaurant, where the scent of scrod throws them off the trail. This aromatic cod dish is in honor of her miscalculation. Baked until golden with crispy breadcrumbs, Parmesan and Pecorino Romano, fresh parsley, and lemon zest, this diverting dinner will summon all your guests to the table.

SERVES 4 TO 6

2 tablespoons unsalted butter, melted, plus more softened for greasing the baking dish
2 pounds (907 g) cod filets
1¼ teaspoons salt, divided
¾ teaspoons freshly ground black pepper, divided
1½ cups (102 g) panko breadcrumbs
½ cup (57 g) grated Parmesan cheese
½ cup (57 g) grated Pecorino Romano cheese
¼ cup (12 g) fresh Italian parsley, finely chopped
Grated zest from 2 lemons
2 tablespoons freshly squeezed lemon juice
1 teaspoon garlic powder
Lemon wedges, for garnish

1 Preheat the oven to 400°F (204°C) and lightly grease a 9 x 13-inch baking dish with butter.

2 Cut the cod into four even-size filets, about 1 inch thick. Place them into the prepared baking dish and sprinkle ½ teaspoon of the salt and ¼ teaspoon of the black pepper over the filets. Turn the filets over, then season them with an additional ½ teaspoon of salt and ¼ teaspoon of pepper. Set aside.

3 In a medium bowl, stir together the breadcrumbs, Parmesan, Pecorino Romano, parsley, lemon zest, lemon juice, garlic powder, and the remaining ¼ teaspoon of salt and ¼ teaspoon of pepper. While stirring, slowly add the 2 tablespoons butter, tossing and coating the crumbs evenly.

4 Use your hands to cover the filets with a generous layer of the breadcrumb mixture, pressing gently so it adheres to the tops and sides of the fish. Continue until all the breadcrumb mixture is used, then gather any loose crumbs in the baking dish and press them onto the fish.

5 Bake for 18 to 20 minutes, until the breadcrumbs are golden and the fish reaches an internal temperature of 140° to 145°F (60° to 63°C) on a digital food thermometer. Let rest for 5 minutes, then garnish with lemon wedges and serve hot. Bone Appetit!

"I smell . . . scrod. Scrod, you know, it's a bottom dweller. You cook it sometimes with lovely breadcrumbs, little bit of margarine."
—MARY SANDERSON

"You whining coward of a vampire who prowls the night killing rats and poodles!"
—LESTAT DE LIONCOURT

LOUIS'S RAT-ATOUILLE

INTERVIEW WITH THE VAMPIRE (1994)

Louis is having a rough time adjusting to his new life as a vampire. He refuses to feed on humans and is wracked with guilt over taking innocent lives. Instead, he lives on a desperate diet of rats and other small animals throughout the night. Surviving as a pacifist vampire is not easy, so this is a vegetarian dish that Louis—and everyone—can enjoy. This visually stunning French Provençal entrée is dressed to impress. A rainbow spiral of colorful veggies—green zucchini, yellow squash, purple Japanese eggplant, and red and orange bell pepper—rests on a bed of zesty marinara, baked until bubbly. Finished with thin strips of fresh basil, this rat-free rat-atouille is a true mouse-terpiece.

SERVES 4 TO 6

FOR THE SLICED VEGETABLES

1 medium green zucchini (250 g)
1 medium yellow squash (220 g)
1 medium purple Japanese eggplant (170 g)
1 medium red bell pepper (170 g)
1 medium orange bell pepper (170 g)

FOR THE SAUCE

2 tablespoons extra-virgin olive oil, plus more for brushing
1 medium yellow onion (360 g), chopped
1 red bell pepper (170 g), chopped
3 large garlic cloves (15 g), finely chopped
1 (15-ounce/425 g) can crushed tomatoes
2 tablespoons chopped fresh basil leaves, plus more to chiffonade for garnish (see Note)
1 tablespoon tomato paste
2 teaspoons salt, divided
½ teaspoon freshly ground black pepper
½ teaspoon dried oregano
½ teaspoon dried thyme
½ teaspoon sugar
⅛ teaspoon red pepper flakes

1 Preheat the oven to 375°F (191°C).

2 **PREPARE THE VEGETABLES:** Using a mandoline or sharp knife, cut the zucchini, squash, eggplant, red bell pepper, and orange bell pepper into ⅛-inch slices. Set aside.

3 **MAKE THE SAUCE:** Place a large skillet over medium heat. When the skillet is hot (see Notes, page 27), drizzle in the olive oil. Add the onion and chopped red bell pepper and cook for 7 to 9 minutes, until softened. Add the garlic and cook for 1 minute. Add the tomatoes, basil, tomato paste, 1½ teaspoons of the salt, the black pepper, oregano, thyme, sugar, and red pepper flakes and stir to combine. Bring to a simmer and cook for 12 to 15 minutes. Transfer to a blender and purée until smooth.

4 Pour the puréed sauce into a round baking dish 9 to 10 inches wide and spread into an even layer. Begin stacking the sliced vegetables vertically around the edge of the dish, alternating colors, and continuing until the entire dish is full of tightly stacked vegetables. Lightly brush the vegetables with olive oil, then sprinkle the remaining ½ teaspoon of salt evenly over the top. Cover the dish and bake for 45 to 50 minutes. Let cool for 5 minutes, then garnish with a chiffonade of basil. Bone Appetit!

NOTE

To chiffonade basil, stack several fresh leaves and roll them up like a burrito. With a sharp knife, cut the roll into thin strips, creating ribbons of basil to use for garnish.

VERY SCARY LAMB CHOPS WITH ROSEMARY AND SEA SALT

IT
(2017)

Mike Hanlon loathes working in the slaughterhouse on his family's lamb farm. He's a quiet teenager with a compassionate nature, too scared to take an animal's life. But after he and his six best friends in The Losers Club valiantly defeat Pennywise in a bloody battle in the sewers beneath the city of Derry, Maine, Mike evolves into a confident, brave young adult. To celebrate his courage and triumph over his fears, these charred chops are bold and tangy, and they don't clown around. Marinated with garlic and fresh rosemary, then pan-seared until juicy and tender—if you're looking for a quick and easy gourmet entrée to impress your friends, this is *It*.

SERVES 4 TO 6

- ¼ cup (59 ml) distilled white vinegar
- 2 tablespoons extra-virgin olive oil
- 1 tablespoon finely chopped fresh rosemary
- 3 large garlic cloves (15 g), finely chopped
- 2 teaspoons salt
- 1 teaspoon freshly ground black pepper
- 4 to 6 lamb rib chops
- 1 tablespoon unsalted butter

1. In a small bowl, whisk together the vinegar, olive oil, rosemary, garlic, salt, and pepper until evenly blended.

2. Place the lamb chops into a large zip-top plastic bag. Pour in the marinade, then gently knead the bag to coat the chops evenly. Remove the air from the bag, then seal it closed and refrigerate for at least 1 hour or up to overnight.

3. Remove the bag from the refrigerator and let rest at room temperature for 20 minutes.

4. Place a large skillet or grill pan over medium-high heat. When hot (see Notes, page 27), remove the chops from the bag and lay them flat in the skillet. Reserve the remaining marinade and set the bag aside. Cook the chops for 2 to 4 minutes per side, until they develop a deep golden brown crust and reach an internal temperature of 125°F (52°C) on a digital food thermometer for medium-rare. Transfer the chops to a plate, cover tightly with foil, and let rest for 5 minutes.

5. While the chops are resting, pour the remaining marinade from the bag into a small saucepan and set over medium heat. Add the butter and bring to a simmer. Cook for 1 to 2 minutes, until the marinade thickens slightly, then remove from the heat. Transfer to a small bowl.

6. Serve the lamb chops hot, with the marinade on the side for dipping, if desired. Bone Appetit!

“Maybe It knows what scares us most, and that’s what we see.”

—MIKE HANLON

"They're only noodles,
Michael."
—DAVID

DECEIVING CHINESE TAKEOUT NOODLES WITH SHIITAKE MUSHROOM WORMS

THE LOST BOYS
(1987)

Follow David and his mischievous friends to a midnight gathering in their hidden vampire's lair. Just remember: don't believe everything you see there. If you're handed a takeout container of rice that suddenly turns into maggots, it's just a hallucination—vampires like to trick your mind. Thankfully, these Chinese takeout noodles are not an illusion. They may look like worms, but this garlicky udon dish happens to be vegetarian. Made with sautéed shiitake mushrooms, green bell peppers, mung bean sprouts, and scallions, this deceptively delicious dinner pairs exquisitely with a bloodred cocktail (see page 127) and a roomful of flickering candles.

SERVES 3 TO 4

FOR THE SAUCE

- 2 tablespoons soy sauce
- 2 tablespoons oyster sauce
- 2 teaspoons rice vinegar
- 1 teaspoon dark brown sugar
- 1 teaspoon sesame oil
- 1 teaspoon sriracha
- ¼ teaspoon ground ginger

FOR THE STIR-FRY

- 16 ounces (454 g) fresh udon noodles
- 2 tablespoons vegetable oil
- 3 cups (226 g) shiitake mushrooms, thinly sliced
- ½ green bell pepper (80 g), thinly sliced
- 3 scallions (70 g), thinly sliced, white and green parts divided
- 1 cup (100 g) mung bean sprouts
- 3 large garlic cloves (15 g), finely chopped

1. **MAKE THE SAUCE:** In a small bowl or measuring cup, combine the soy sauce, oyster sauce, vinegar, brown sugar, sesame oil, sriracha, and ginger and stir until blended. Set aside.

2. **MAKE THE STIR-FRY:** Bring a medium pot of water to a boil. Add the udon noodles and cook for 1 to 2 minutes, until the noodles separate and soften. Drain the noodles and rinse with cold water. Set aside.

3. Place a large wok or skillet over medium heat and swirl in the vegetable oil. When the oil starts to shimmer, add the mushrooms, bell pepper, and the white parts of the scallions. Stir to combine and cook for 5 to 6 minutes, until softened, stirring often. Then add the udon noodles, mung bean sprouts, garlic, and the prepared sauce, tossing to combine. Cook for 3 minutes, stirring gently to avoid breaking the noodles, then remove from the heat. Serve immediately, and garnish with the green parts of the scallions. Bone Appetit!

SHARP SKEWERS WITH CAJUN SHRIMP AND PEPPERS

A NIGHTMARE ON ELM STREET (1984)

Freddy Kreuger, sadistic serial killer who haunts and murders people in their dreams, wears a tattered red and green striped sweater, an old brown fedora, and a glove with razor-sharp blades on the fingers. Channeling Freddy's deadly demeanor, this recipe is as bold and blistering as his lethal blades. Fresh shrimp are marinated in a zesty Cajun sauce, then grilled on metal skewers with sliced red and green peppers to match Freddy's sinister sweater. Garnished with parsley and a squeeze of lemon, these spicy skewers are a nightmare come true.

SERVES 4

- 2 teaspoons smoked paprika
- 2 teaspoons garlic powder
- 1 teaspoon salt
- 1 teaspoon onion powder
- 1 teaspoon dried oregano
- 1 teaspoon dried thyme
- 1 teaspoon freshly ground black pepper
- 1 teaspoon ground cayenne pepper
- Grated zest from 1 lemon
- 2 tablespoons freshly squeezed lemon juice
- 2 tablespoons extra-virgin olive oil
- 1 pound (454 g) jumbo shrimp (about 18 to 20), peeled and deveined
- 1 red bell pepper
- 1 green bell pepper
- 6 to 8 metal skewers (about 8 inches long)
- Chopped fresh parsley, for garnish
- Lemon wedges, for serving (optional)

1. In a small bowl, stir together the paprika, garlic powder, salt, onion powder, oregano, thyme, black pepper, and cayenne pepper until evenly blended. Add the lemon zest, lemon juice, and olive oil, and stir to make a smooth paste.

2. Place the shrimp into a large zip-top bag. Add the marinade, then knead the bag to coat the shrimp evenly. Remove the air from the bag, then seal it closed and refrigerate for 15 to 30 minutes.

3. Discard the seeds and stems from the bell peppers, then cut the peppers into pieces about ½ inch wide by 2 inches long. Note that if the pieces are too large, they prevent the skewers from cooking evenly.

4. Assemble each skewer by inserting one shrimp, then one red pepper, then one green pepper, and repeat the pattern until the skewer is filled. Repeat with the remaining skewers.

5. Heat a large grill or skillet over medium heat. When hot, grill the skewers for 2 to 3 minutes per side, until the shrimp is pink and opaque throughout. Garnish with chopped parsley and serve immediately with lemon wedges, if desired. Bone Appetit!

"He scraped his fingernails along things. Actually, they were more like finger-knives or something."
—NANCY THOMPSON

POTIONS, DRINKS, AND BOO-ZY COCKTAILS

YOU DON'T NEED TO BE AN ACTUAL WITCH TO CRAFT A MAGIC POTION, YOU JUST NEED A SOLID RECIPE.

In these enchanting pages, you'll learn how to brew some of the most powerful (and delicious) spells ever created. One sip of the Potion of Eternal Youth (page 117) inspired by **DEATH BECOMES HER** will restore your beauty and keep you young until the end of time. The sage-smoked Love Potion (page 113) in homage to **THE CRAFT** causes your secret crush to fall desperately head over heels for you. And the bloodred Lazarus Potion (page 110) paying tribute to **CASPER** can resurrect the dead and bring ghosts back to life. From batch cocktails for parties like Bloodbath Punch (page 127) evoking the terror of **IT** to nonalcoholic incantations like Nancy's Stay-Awake Salted Caramel Latte (page 137) honoring **A NIGHTMARE ON ELM STREET**, there are magical libations for every situation!

"I only like all-natural foods and beverages, organically grown, with no preservatives. Are you sure they're real lemons?"
—GIRL SCOUT

WEDNESDAY & PUGSLEY'S POISON LEMONADE

THE ADDAMS FAMILY (1991)

Wednesday and Pugsley Addams clearly inherited the cooking gene from Grandmama. After their parents are swindled out of their entire fortune and evicted from their ancestral home, the kids set up a lemonade stand to help raise money for the family. While their recipe includes traditional Addams ingredients like arsenic and cyanide, we've adapted this version to be less lethal. Made with fresh lemon juice and a zesty peach-ginger simple syrup, this benign beverage gets its striking blue hue from all-natural spirulina powder. Garnished with a spooky skull-and-crossbones cocktail pick and a lemon slice, this refreshing drink will make Grandmama proud.

SERVES 6 TO 8

FOR THE PEACH-GINGER SIMPLE SYRUP

- 1 cup (237 ml) water
- 1 cup (198 g) granulated sugar
- 2 (15-ounce/425 g) cans peach halves, drained and chopped (see Notes)
- 2 ounces (57 g) fresh ginger root (about 4 inches), sliced

FOR THE LEMONADE

- 4 cups (946 ml) water
- 1¼ cups (296 ml) Peach-Ginger Simple Syrup
- ¾ cup (177 ml) freshly squeezed lemon juice (4 to 5 lemons)
- 1 teaspoon blue spirulina powder (see Notes)
- Ice, for serving
- Dry ice, for garnish (optional; see Notes)
- Lemon slices, for garnish
- Skull-and-crossbones cocktail picks

1 **MAKE THE PEACH-GINGER SIMPLE SYRUP:** In a small saucepan, combine the water, sugar, peaches, and ginger. Place the pan over medium heat and bring to a simmer, stirring occasionally. Once simmering, cover the pan, reduce the heat to the lowest setting, and simmer gently for 10 minutes. Then turn off the heat and let the mixture rest for 15 minutes. Strain using a fine-mesh strainer, then transfer the syrup to a sealed container and refrigerate for 1 to 2 hours, until chilled. The syrup can keep in the fridge for up to 2 weeks. This recipe makes about 1½ cups syrup, enough for one pitcher of lemonade.

2 **MAKE THE LEMONADE:** In a large pitcher, combine the water, the peach-ginger simple syrup, lemon juice, and spirulina powder and stir until blended. Fill the pitcher with ice and stir briefly. If desired, add dry ice just before serving (see Notes). Garnish each glass with ice, a lemon slice, and a skull-and-crossbones cocktail pick. Bone Appetit!

NOTES

For the peaches, be sure to buy canned fruit with 100% juice, rather than syrup.

If desired, reserve the leftover peaches for future use: as a topping for ice cream or pancakes, or simply enjoyed by the spoonful.

Blue spirulina powder is available in natural food stores and online.

Important: Do not ingest dry ice cubes. Dry ice is safe to use in drinks but should never be consumed. Be sure to wait for the dry ice to dissolve before drinking.

LAZARUS POTION

CASPER
(1995)

Casper's father secretly invented a machine that can resurrect the dead. Hidden within an underground chamber deep below Whipstaff Manor, the Lazarus Machine is the only thing that can turn Casper back into a boy again. This remarkable invention requires a rare potion to function—and there's only one vial left. In the spirit of his ingenuity, this revitalizing, ruby-red cocktail is a haunting riff on a classic Cosmopolitan. Simply shaken over ice with vodka, pomegranate juice, orange liqueur, lime juice, and grenadine, this lustrous libation is powerful enough to bring any party back to life.

SERVES 10 TO 11

1¾ cups plus 2 tablespoons (444 ml) vodka

1¾ cups plus 2 tablespoons (444 ml) unsweetened pomegranate juice

1¼ cups (296 ml) orange liqueur, such as Triple Sec or Cointreau

1¼ cups (296 ml) freshly squeezed lime juice (12 to 14 limes)

1¼ cups (296 ml) grenadine

Ice, for shaking

Maraschino cherries, for garnish

Lime twists, for garnish

In a large pitcher or drink dispenser, combine the vodka, pomegranate juice, orange liqueur, lime juice, and grenadine. Keep refrigerated until ready to serve. For each serving, pour 6 ounces (¾ cup) of the mixture into a cocktail shaker, then fill the shaker with ice and shake vigorously for 20 seconds. Strain into a rounded glass, such as a Florence flask, Scotch whisky glass, or stemless wineglass, then garnish with a maraschino cherry and a lime twist. Bone Appetit!

"Careful—that's what makes the whole thing work. Kind of an instant primordial soup mix. It's what brings ghosts back to life. Just enough for one."

—CASPER

LAZARUS POTION SINGLE COCKTAIL RECIPE

SERVES 1

- 1½ ounces (45 ml) vodka
- 1½ ounces (45 ml) unsweetened pomegranate juice
- 1 ounce (30 ml) orange liqueur, such as Triple Sec or Cointreau
- 1 ounce (30 ml) freshly squeezed lime juice
- 1 ounce (30 ml) grenadine
- Ice, for shaking
- Maraschino cherry, for garnish
- Lime twist, for garnish

In a cocktail shaker, combine the vodka, pomegranate juice, orange liqueur, lime juice, and grenadine. Fill the shaker with ice and shake vigorously for 20 seconds. Strain into a rounded glass, such as a Florence flask, Scotch whisky glass, or stemless wineglass. Garnish with a maraschino cherry and a lime twist. Bone Appetit!

LOVE POTION

THE CRAFT
(1996)

After discovering their supernatural powers, Sarah, Nancy, Bonnie, and Rochelle venture into the woods to perform their first coven ritual. They burn sage and drink from a goblet of red wine with a drop of blood from each of their fingers. The girls conjure forces of beauty, power, and revenge—while Sarah casts a love spell on her crush, Chris Hooker. This captivating cocktail—a witchy riff on a New York Sour served in a sage-smoked glass—might not require magic, but it's sure to make your guests fall in love with you.

SERVES 10 TO 11

FOR THE SIMPLE SYRUP (SEE NOTES)

1 cup (237 ml) water
1 cup (198 g) granulated sugar

FOR THE COCKTAIL

2½ cups (591 ml) bourbon or rye whiskey
1¼ cups (296 ml) freshly squeezed lemon juice (6 to 8 lemons)
1¼ cups (296 ml) Simple Syrup
20 dashes Angostura bitters
Dried whole sage leaves (see Notes)
Ice, for shaking and serving
1¼ cups (296 ml) dry red wine, such as Cabernet Sauvignon or Malbec
Strawberries cut into heart shapes, for garnish
Cocktail picks, for garnish

1 **MAKE THE SIMPLE SYRUP:** In a small saucepan, combine the water and sugar. Place the pan over medium-low heat and stir until the sugar dissolves. Remove from the heat and let cool for 15 minutes. Transfer the syrup to a sealed container and refrigerate for 1 to 2 hours, until chilled. The syrup can keep in the fridge for up to 2 weeks. This recipe makes about 1½ cups syrup, enough for 10 to 11 cocktails.

2 **MAKE THE COCKTAILS:** In a large pitcher or drink dispenser, combine the bourbon, lemon juice, simple syrup, and bitters. Keep refrigerated until ready to serve.

3 For each serving, just before serving, place a 4-inch square of aluminum foil on a heatproof surface, such as a ceramic plate. Light a dried sage leaf on fire, let it burn for a few seconds, then gently blow out the flame. Place the smoking leaf on the foil, then invert a rocks glass or old-fashioned glass and place it over the leaf, filling the glass with smoke. Discard the burnt sage leaf when ready to use the glass.

4 Pour 4 ounces (½ cup) of the bourbon mixture into a cocktail shaker, then fill the shaker with ice and shake vigorously for 20 seconds. Place a few ice cubes into the smoked serving glass, then strain the cocktail into the glass. Gently pour 1 ounce of wine over the back of a spoon into the glass, allowing the wine to float on top, then garnish the glass with a dried sage leaf and a strawberry heart on a pick.

NOTES

To make a quick simple syrup without using a stove, combine equal parts water and granulated sugar in a measuring cup and stir until the sugar dissolves.

Dried whole sage leaves are available online or in health food stores and natural markets. Alternatively, you can dry your own by placing fresh sage leaves on a parchment-lined baking sheet and baking in the oven at 175°F (80°C) for 30 to 45 minutes, until dry and crisp.

LOVE POTION
SINGLE COCKTAIL RECIPE

SERVES 1

- 2 ounces (60 ml) bourbon or rye whiskey
- 1 ounce (30 ml) freshly squeezed lemon juice
- 1 ounce (30 ml) simple syrup (page 113)
- 2 dashes Angostura bitters
- Ice, for shaking and serving
- 2 dried sage leaves (see Notes, page 113)
- 1 ounce (30 ml) dry red wine, such as Cabernet Sauvignon or Malbec
- Strawberry cut into a heart shape, for garnish
- Cocktail pick, for garnish

1 In a cocktail shaker, combine the bourbon, lemon juice, simple syrup, and bitters. Fill the shaker with ice and shake vigorously for 20 seconds. Set aside.

2 Place a 4-inch square of aluminum foil on a heatproof surface, such as a ceramic plate. Light a dried sage leaf on fire, let it burn for a few seconds, then gently blow out the flame. Place the smoking leaf on the foil, then invert a rocks glass or old-fashioned glass and place it over the leaf, filling the glass with smoke. Discard the burnt sage leaf.

3 Flip over the smoked glass, add a few ice cubes, then strain the cocktail into the glass. Gently pour the wine over the back of a spoon into the glass, allowing the wine to float on top. Garnish with the remaining sage leaf and the strawberry heart on a pick. Bone Appetit!

"I drink of my sisters, and I ask to love myself more and to allow myself to be loved more by others . . . especially Chris Hooker."
—SARAH BAILEY

"Drink that potion and you'll never grow even one day older."

—LISLE VON RHUMAN

POTION OF ETERNAL YOUTH

DEATH BECOMES HER
(1992)

If you were given the chance to live forever, would you accept? Madeline Ashton jumps at the opportunity when she's tempted by Lisle Von Rhuman, who has a crystal vial of shimmering pink potion that brings eternal youth. After Madeline drinks the elixir, the wrinkles on her face disappear, and her body transforms into a younger, curvier version of herself. Just like the glowing tincture in the movie, this cocktail offers a taste of magic. Made with tequila, lime juice, and orange liqueur, this life-changing potion is sweetened with strawberry simple syrup and colored with red dragon fruit purée. Finished with a splash of club soda and a pinch of edible pink shimmer powder, this rejuvenating refreshment is impossible to resist. Siempre viva!

SERVES 10 TO 11

FOR THE STRAWBERRY SIMPLE SYRUP

- 1½ cups (355 ml) water
- 1½ cups (297 g) granulated sugar
- 1 pound (454 g) strawberries, fresh or frozen

FOR THE COCKTAIL

- 1¾ cups plus 2 tablespoons (444 ml) silver tequila
- 1¾ cups plus 2 tablespoons (444 ml) freshly squeezed lime juice (16 to 18 limes)
- 1¾ cups plus 2 tablespoons (444 ml) Strawberry Simple Syrup
- ¾ cup plus 3 tablespoons (222 ml) orange liqueur, such as Triple Sec or Cointreau
- 2½ tablespoons seedless red dragon fruit purée (see Notes)
- Edible pink shimmer powder (optional)
- Ice, for shaking
- 1¾ cups plus 2 tablespoons (444 ml) club soda

1. **MAKE THE STRAWBERRY SIMPLE SYRUP:** In a small saucepan, combine the water, sugar, and strawberries. Place the pan over medium heat and bring to a simmer, stirring occasionally. Once simmering, cover the pan, reduce the heat to the lowest setting, and simmer gently for 10 minutes. Then turn off the heat and let the mixture rest for 15 minutes. Strain using a fine-mesh strainer (see Notes), then transfer the syrup to a sealed container and refrigerate for 1 to 2 hours, until chilled. The syrup can keep in the fridge for up to 2 weeks. This recipe makes about 2 cups of strawberry simple syrup, enough for 10 to 11 cocktails.

2. **MAKE THE COCKTAILS:** In a large pitcher or drink dispenser, combine the tequila, lime juice, strawberry syrup, orange liqueur, and dragon fruit purée. Keep refrigerated until ready to serve. For each serving, pour 6 ounces (¾ cup) of the mixture into a cocktail shaker, and add, if using, a pinch of pink shimmer powder, then fill the shaker with ice and shake vigorously for 20 seconds. Strain into a champagne flute, then add 1½ ounces of club soda. Bone Appetit!

NOTES

Red dragon fruit purée is found in the frozen section of many natural food stores. If it contains seeds, strain out the seeds before use.

If desired, reserve the leftover strawberries for future use: as a topping for ice cream or pancakes, or simply enjoyed by the spoonful.

POTION OF ETERNAL YOUTH SINGLE COCKTAIL RECIPE

SERVES 1

- 1½ ounces (45 ml) silver tequila
- 1½ ounces (45 ml) freshly squeezed lime juice
- 1½ ounces (45 ml) Strawberry Simple Syrup (page 117)
- ¾ ounce (25 ml) orange liqueur, such as Triple Sec or Cointreau
- ¾ teaspoon seedless red dragon fruit purée (see Notes, page 117)
- Edible pink shimmer powder (optional)
- Ice, for shaking
- 1½ ounces (45 ml) club soda

In a cocktail shaker, combine the tequila, lime juice, strawberry syrup, orange liqueur, dragon fruit purée, and, if using, a pinch of pink shimmer powder. Fill the shaker with ice and shake vigorously for 20 seconds. Strain into a champagne flute, then add the club soda. Bone Appetit!

HOLY WATER ELIXIR

Peter Vincent is a broke, washed-up actor who once played a vampire hunter in a series of low-budget horror films. When Charley's friends pay him five hundred dollars to investigate Jerry Dandridge at his home and determine whether he's a vampire, he brings a fake vial of holy water, since he doesn't believe in the supernatural. Jerry doesn't react after drinking the phony tap water, so everyone—except for Charley—is convinced that he passed the test. If only they had given him something more divine, like this miraculous Holy Water Elixir, the movie might have ended much sooner. This crystal clear, chocolate-mint cocktail is blessed with flavor. Made with your favorite vodka, crème de cacao, and crème de menthe liqueur, no vampire would dare touch this with a ten-foot stake.

SERVES 10 TO 11

1¼ cups (296 ml) vodka

1¼ cups (296 ml) clear crème de menthe liqueur

1¼ cups (296 ml) clear crème de cacao liqueur

Ice, for shaking

Chocolate hearts, for garnish

Crucifix-shaped cocktail picks, for garnish

Fresh mint leaves, for garnish

In a large pitcher or drink dispenser, combine the vodka, crème de menthe, and crème de cacao. Keep refrigerated until ready to serve. For each serving, pour 3 ounces (6 tablespoons) of the mixture into a cocktail shaker, then fill the shaker with ice and shake vigorously for 20 seconds. Strain into a coupe glass, then garnish with a chocolate heart on a crucifix-shaped cocktail pick and a mint leaf. Bone Appetit!

HOLY WATER ELIXIR SINGLE COCKTAIL RECIPE

SERVES 1

1 ounce (30 ml) vodka
1 ounce (30 ml) clear crème de menthe liqueur
1 ounce (30 ml) clear crème de cacao liqueur
Ice, for shaking
Chocolate heart, for garnish
Crucifix-shaped cocktail pick, for garnish
Fresh mint leaf, for garnish

In a cocktail shaker, combine the vodka, crème de menthe, and crème de cacao. Fill the shaker with ice and shake vigorously for 20 seconds. Strain into a coupe glass, then garnish with a chocolate heart on a crucifix-shaped cocktail pick and a mint leaf. Bone Appetit!

"You have to have faith for that to work on me."
—JERRY DANDRIDGE

"This is witches' brew. It's a little recipe that I picked up in the sixth century, around King Arthur's time."

—AGGIE CROMWELL

INSTANT WITCHES' BREW CHAI LATTE MIX

HALLOWEENTOWN
(1998)

Between casting spells and paying bills, the modern enchantress doesn't always have time to prepare her brews from scratch. Thankfully, the local grocery stores in Halloweentown carry a microwavable instant witches' brew that cooks in just seconds. Aggie Cromwell uses some when she and her grandchildren—Marnie, Dylan, and Sophie—attempt to bring an ancient talisman back to life to help protect the city from an evil wizard. While their recipe includes ingredients like vampire's fang, hair of a werewolf, and sweat of a ghost, this chai latte version is a bit more approachable. Warm spices like cinnamon, ginger, nutmeg, allspice, cardamom, cloves, and black pepper are blended with sugar, black tea powder, and vanilla nondairy creamer, creating an aromatic mix ready to brew anytime you need to cast a quick spell—just add hot water!

SERVES ABOUT 10

- 1 cup (198 g) granulated sugar
- ½ cup (40 g) powdered milk
- ½ cup (60 g) powdered plain nondairy creamer
- ½ cup (80 g) powdered vanilla nondairy creamer
- ½ cup (40 g) black tea powder (see Note)
- 1 tablespoon ground cinnamon
- 1 teaspoon ground ginger
- ½ teaspoon ground nutmeg
- ½ teaspoon ground allspice
- ½ teaspoon ground cardamom
- ½ teaspoon ground cloves
- ⅛ teaspoon freshly ground black pepper

1. In a medium bowl, combine the sugar, powdered milk, powdered plain nondairy creamer, powdered vanilla nondairy creamer, black tea powder, cinnamon, ginger, nutmeg, allspice, cardamom, cloves, and pepper and whisk together until evenly blended. Transfer to a food processor and pulse until finely ground. Store the chai latte mix in an airtight container at room temperature for up to 6 months.

2. To prepare one serving, combine 4 tablespoons of instant chai latte mix with 8 ounces boiling water. Stir to combine and serve hot. Bone Appetit!

NOTE

Black tea powder is available in natural food stores and online.

LESTAT'S BLOODY MARY

INTERVIEW WITH THE VAMPIRE

(1994)

Lestat de Lioncourt is a seductive vampire who has preyed on humans for more than two hundred years. Sexy and charismatic, he thrives as a merciless night-hunter in the bayous of New Orleans. Unlike his protégé, Louis, who feels deeply ashamed hurting innocent people, Lestat loves being a vampire. To commemorate his insatiable thirst, this killer cocktail is a vampire's unholy grail. Spicy and savory—made with vodka, tomato juice, lemon and lime juice, horseradish, Worcestershire sauce, and Tabasco—this bold Bloody Mary will quench the thirst of humans and vampires alike.

SERVES 6

- **5¾ cups (1360 ml) tomato juice**
- **¼ cup (60 ml) freshly squeezed lemon juice (1 to 2 lemons)**
- **¼ cup (60 ml) freshly squeezed lime juice (2 to 3 limes)**
- **1½ tablespoons Worcestershire sauce**
- **4 teaspoons prepared horseradish**
- **3 teaspoons Tabasco sauce**
- **3 teaspoons celery salt**
- **2½ teaspoons freshly ground black pepper**
- **9 ounces (266 ml) vodka**
- **Ice, for serving**

GARNISH SUGGESTIONS

- **Tajín seasoning, to rim the glasses (see Note)**
- **Lemon wedges**
- **Celery stalks**
- **Pimento-stuffed green olives**
- **Fresh basil leaves or dill**
- **Gherkins or small pickles**
- **Cocktail onions**
- **Sliced bacon**
- **Grilled prawns (page 48)**

1 In a pitcher, combine the tomato juice, lemon juice, lime juice, Worcestershire sauce, horseradish, Tabasco sauce, celery salt, and pepper and stir until blended. Refrigerate for 3 to 4 hours, until chilled, or until ready to serve. The mix will keep in the fridge for up to 3 days.

2 For each serving, pour 1½ ounces (45 ml) vodka into a tall glass. Fill the glass with ice, then add 8 ounces (237 ml) of Bloody Mary mix and stir to combine. Add desired garnishes and serve. Bone Appetit!

NOTE

To rim a serving glass with Tajín, first pour a few tablespoons of Tajín onto a small, flat plate. Wet the rim of a glass by rubbing it with a cut wedge of lemon, then dip the rim in the Tajín, coating it evenly.

"Lord, what I wouldn't give for a drop of good old-fashioned Creole blood."

—LESTAT DE LIONCOURT

"You see it? My dad couldn't see it.
I thought I might be crazy."
—BEVERLY MARSH

BLOODBATH PUNCH

IT
(2017)

None of the children in Derry, Maine, are safe—not even at home. Thirteen-year-old Beverly Marsh is hiding in the bathroom, reading an anonymous love letter when fountains of blood erupt from the sink like a volcano, splattering the walls and ceiling and drenching her as she screams in terror. Her father bursts in, but since adults can't perceive the supernatural effects of It, he doesn't see anything wrong. Bleeding with flavor, this boozy bloodbath punch is explosively delicious. Mixed with tart cherry juice and flavors of pineapple, peach, coconut, lime, grenadine, and vanilla, this deceptive drink may look like blood, but it's just an illusion.

SERVES 10 TO 12

- 1½ cups (355 ml) silver rum
- 1½ cups (355 ml) tart cherry juice
- 1½ cups (355 ml) pineapple juice
- ¾ cup (177 ml) peach schnapps
- ¾ cup (177 ml) coconut rum, such as Malibu
- ¾ cup (177 ml) freshly squeezed lime juice (6 to 8 limes)
- 6 tablespoons (89 ml) grenadine
- 1½ teaspoons vanilla extract
- ¼ teaspoon red food dye
- 12 dashes Angostura bitters
- 2¼ cups (532 ml) club soda
- Ice, for serving
- Lime slices, for garnish
- Maraschino cherries, for garnish

1 In a large punch bowl, combine the silver rum, cherry juice, pineapple juice, peach schnapps, coconut rum, lime juice, grenadine, vanilla, red food dye, and Angostura bitters and stir until blended. Keep refrigerated until ready to serve.

2 Just before serving, add the club soda, several cups of ice, and several lime slices. Serve using a ladle and garnish each glass with a lime slice and a cherry. Bone Appetit!

VAMPIRE BLOOD NEGRONI

THE LOST BOYS
(1987)

Michael is peer-pressured by his new friends into drinking from a mysterious bottle—which, unbeknownst to him, is filled with blood. In an attempt to look cool and get closer to his crush, Star, he takes a sip, beginning his transformation into a vampire. Now you can "be one of them," too, with this alluring Vampire Blood Negroni. Shaken with your favorite gin, Campari, and Averna amaro—and appropriately garnished with a blood orange—*thou shalt not* miss out on this ravishing riff on a classic Negroni.

SERVES 10 TO 11

1¼ cups (296 ml) gin
1¼ cups (296 ml) Campari
½ cup plus 2 tablespoons (148 ml) Averna amaro
Ice, for shaking and serving
Blood orange slices, for garnish

In a large pitcher or drink dispenser, combine the gin, Campari, and Averna. Keep refrigerated until ready to serve. For each serving, pour 2½ ounces (5 tablespoons) of the mixture into a cocktail shaker, then fill the shaker with ice and shake vigorously for 20 seconds. Place a few ice cubes into a rocks glass or old-fashioned glass, then strain the cocktail into the glass and garnish with a blood orange slice. Bone Appetit!

SINGLE COCKTAIL RECIPE

SERVES 1

1 ounce (30 ml) gin
1 ounce (30 ml) Campari
½ ounce (15 ml) Averna amaro
Ice, for shaking and serving
Blood orange slice, for garnish

In a cocktail shaker, combine the gin, Campari, and Averna. Fill the shaker with ice and shake vigorously for 20 seconds. Place a few ice cubes into a rocks glass or old-fashioned glass, then strain the cocktail into the glass. Garnish with the blood orange slice. Bone Appetit!

"Drink some of this,
Michael. Be one of us."
—DAVID

"They're coming to get you, Barbra."
—JOHNNY

PASSIONFRUIT ZOMBIE

NIGHT OF THE LIVING DEAD (1968)

Two siblings, Johnny and Barbra, drive three hours to visit their father's grave. After placing a memorial wreath on the tombstone, Johnny teases his sister about being nervous in cemeteries when a zombie suddenly appears, attacking and killing him in a violent struggle. Barbra flees in terror but quickly realizes that nowhere is safe—the undead have begun to rise. Inspired by these cadaverous creatures and the classic tiki cocktail, the Zombie, this delectable drink is fiendishly flavorful. Blended with fresh passion fruit purée and three kinds of rum, then garnished with a spooky zombie-hand-shaped cocktail pick, this beastly beverage is powerful enough to wake the dead.

SERVES 10 TO 11

FOR THE CINNAMON SIMPLE SYRUP

- ½ cup (118 ml) water
- ½ cup (99 g) granulated sugar
- 3 cinnamon sticks

FOR THE COCKTAIL

- 1¾ cups plus 2 tablespoons (444 ml) aged Jamaican rum
- 1¾ cups plus 2 tablespoons (444 ml) Puerto Rican gold rum
- 1¼ cups (296 ml) 151 proof rum
- ¾ cup plus 3 tablespoons (222 ml) freshly squeezed lime juice (8 to 10 limes)
- ½ cup plus 2 tablespoons (148 ml) seedless passion fruit purée (see Note)
- ½ cup plus 2 tablespoons (148 ml) Cinnamon Simple Syrup
- ½ cup plus 2 tablespoons (148 ml) velvet falernum liqueur
- 3 tablespoons plus 1 teaspoon (49 ml) grenadine
- 1¼ teaspoons anise liqueur, such as Pernod or absinthe
- 10 dashes Angostura bitters
- Crushed ice, for serving
- Fresh mint leaves, for garnish
- Maraschino cherries, for garnish
- Orange slices, for garnish
- Skeleton-hand- or zombie-hand-shaped cocktail picks

1 **MAKE THE CINNAMON SIMPLE SYRUP:** In a small saucepan, combine the water, sugar, and cinnamon sticks, using your hands to break up the sticks as you add them to the pan. Place the pan over medium heat and bring to a simmer, stirring occasionally. Once simmering, cover the pan, reduce the heat to the lowest setting, and simmer gently for 10 minutes. Then turn off the heat and let the mixture rest for 15 minutes. Strain using a fine-mesh strainer, then transfer the syrup to a sealed container and refrigerate for 1 to 2 hours, until chilled. The syrup can keep in the fridge for up to 2 weeks. This recipe makes about ¾ cup of cinnamon simple syrup, enough for 10 to 11 cocktails.

2 **MAKE THE COCKTAILS:** In a large pitcher or drink dispenser, combine the Jamaican rum, gold rum, 151 proof rum, lime juice, passion fruit purée, cinnamon syrup, velvet falernum, grenadine, anise liqueur, and Angostura bitters. Keep refrigerated until ready to serve. For each serving, fill a tall glass, such as a hurricane glass, with ice, then add 8 ounces (1 cup) of the cocktail mixture. Garnish the glass with mint, a cherry, an orange slice, and a skeleton-hand- or zombie-hand-shaped cocktail pick. Bone Appetit!

NOTE

Seedless passion fruit purée is available in the frozen section of many natural food stores.

PASSIONFRUIT ZOMBIE SINGLE COCKTAIL RECIPE

SERVES 1

- 1½ ounces (45 ml) aged Jamaican rum
- 1½ ounces (45 ml) Puerto Rican gold rum
- 1 ounce (30 ml) 151 proof rum
- ¾ ounce (25 ml) freshly squeezed lime juice
- ½ ounce (15 ml) seedless passion fruit purée (see Note, page 131)
- ½ ounce (15 ml) Cinnamon Simple Syrup (page 131)
- ½ ounce (15 ml) velvet falernum liqueur
- 1 teaspoon grenadine
- ⅛ teaspoon anise liqueur, such as Pernod or absinthe
- Dash of Angostura bitters
- ¾ cup (177 ml) crushed ice for blending, plus more for serving
- Fresh mint leaves, for garnish
- Maraschino cherry, for garnish
- Orange slice, for garnish
- Skeleton-hand- or zombie-hand-shaped cocktail pick

In a blender, combine the Jamaican rum, gold rum, 151 proof rum, lime juice, passion fruit purée, cinnamon syrup, velvet falernum, grenadine, anise liqueur, the dash of Angostura bitters, and ice. Blend for 5 seconds, then pour into a tall glass, such as a hurricane glass. Fill the glass with additional ice, then garnish with mint, a cherry, an orange slice, and a skeleton-hand- or zombie-hand-shaped cocktail pick. Bone Appetit!

KATRINA'S NIGHTTIME BREW

SLEEPY HOLLOW

(1999)

Ichabod Crane is recovering in bed after being stabbed by the Headless Horseman. He's feverish and delirious, and his crush, Katrina Van Tassel, is preparing a special sleeping potion to help him recover. In her candlelit kitchen, she casts a healing spell over a bubbling cauldron of exotic ingredients that put him to sleep after just one sip. The next time you're looking to unwind, this calming brew will soothe your soul. Spicy cinnamon sticks, cloves, and star anise are gently simmered until warm and fragrant, then stirred with freshly squeezed lemon juice, honey, bourbon, and spiced rum. This relaxing blend doesn't contain an obscure raven's claw like Katrina's, but it'll send you to dreamland just as quickly.

SERVES 10

- 7½ cups (1774 ml) water
- 5 cinnamon sticks, plus more for garnish
- 10 whole cloves
- 5 star anise pods
- 1¾ cups plus 2 tablespoons (444 ml) honey
- 1¼ cups (296 ml) bourbon
- 1¼ cups (296 ml) spiced rum
- ¾ cup plus 2 tablespoons (207 ml) freshly squeezed lemon juice (4 to 6 lemons)
- Lemon slices, for garnish

In a medium saucepan, combine the water, cinnamon sticks, cloves, and anise pods. Cover, bring to a boil over high heat, then reduce the heat to low and simmer for 8 to 10 minutes. Reduce the heat to the lowest setting, then add the honey, bourbon, rum, and lemon juice and stir to combine. Add a few lemon slices for garnish, cover, and keep warm. Serve using a ladle and garnish the glasses with lemon slices and cinnamon sticks. Bone Appetit!

KATRINA'S NIGHTTIME BREW SINGLE COCKTAIL RECIPE

SERVES 1

¾ cup (177 ml) water
1 cinnamon stick
2 whole cloves
1 star anise pod
1½ ounces (45 ml) honey
1 ounce (30 ml) bourbon
1 ounce (30 ml) spiced rum
4 teaspoons (20 ml) freshly squeezed lemon juice
Lemon slice, for garnish

1 In a small saucepan, combine the water, cinnamon stick, cloves, and anise pod. Cover, bring to a boil over high heat, then reduce heat to the lowest setting and simmer for 8 to 10 minutes.

2 While the water is simmering, pour the honey, bourbon, rum, and lemon juice into a serving mug.

3 Once the water is done simmering, remove the whole spices with a slotted spoon, reserving the cinnamon stick for garnish, and pour the hot water into the prepared mug. Stir until the honey dissolves, then add the reserved cinnamon stick and a lemon slice for garnish and serve hot. Bone Appetit!

"Drink this down. It will make you sleep."

—KATRINA VAN TASSEL

"Whatever you do, don't fall asleep."

—NANCY THOMPSON

NANCY'S STAY-AWAKE SALTED CARAMEL LATTE

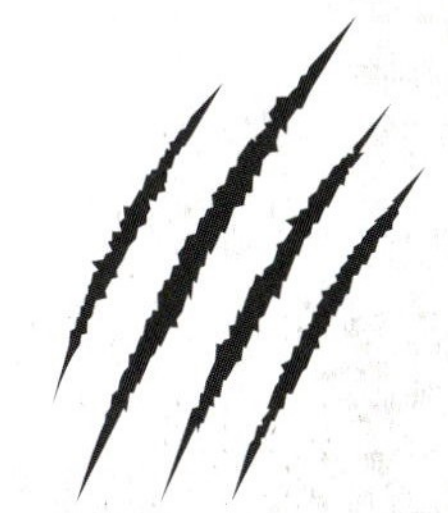

A NIGHTMARE ON ELM STREET
(1984)

Nancy Thompson needs to stay awake to stay alive. Her friends were murdered in their dreams by the sadistic serial killer Freddy Krueger, and she's terrified that if she falls asleep, she'll become his next victim. Nancy fights to stay up for seven days, relying on endless cups of coffee and caffeine pills to keep her eyes open. This dreamy, stay-awake latte will do just that. Rich salted caramel with hints of vanilla is stirred into a hot cup of your favorite coffee, then topped with whipped cream and drizzled with more caramel. Insomnia has never tasted so good.

SERVES 1

FOR THE SALTED CARAMEL

½ cup (99 g) granulated sugar
1 tablespoon light corn syrup
¼ cup (59 ml) heavy cream
1 tablespoon unsalted butter
½ teaspoon salt
½ teaspoon vanilla extract

FOR THE COFFEE

6 ounces (177 ml) hot brewed coffee
½ cup (118 ml) milk of choice, such as oat or whole milk
2 tablespoons Salted Caramel, plus more for drizzling (optional)
Whipped cream, homemade (see page 183) or store-bought, for garnish (optional)

1 **MAKE THE SALTED CARAMEL:** In a small saucepan, combine the sugar, 1 tablespoon plus 1 teaspoon water, and the corn syrup. Set over medium heat and cook for 8 to 10 minutes, stirring often, until amber-colored. Remove from the heat and add the heavy cream, butter, salt, and vanilla. Stir until smooth and blended, then either use immediately or transfer to a heatproof sealed container and place in the fridge to cool. The caramel will stay fresh for up to 1 week in the fridge—note that the caramel thickens when refrigerated, so it must be warmed briefly in the microwave until it reaches a pourable consistency. This recipe makes about 1 cup of caramel, enough for 4 to 6 servings.

2 **MAKE THE COFFEE:** Prepare a 6-ounce cup of hot coffee using the method of your choice.

3 While the coffee is brewing, whisk together the milk and the salted caramel in a small saucepan. Set the heat to medium-low and cook, whisking often, until the milk becomes steamy and begins to thicken and foam.

4 Drizzle about 1 tablespoon of the warm caramel sauce into the serving mug, coating the sides, then add the hot coffee and the hot foamy milk. If desired, top with whipped cream and a drizzle of caramel sauce. Bone Appetit!

MIDNIGHT MARGARITAS WITH LIME AND COCONUT

PRACTICAL MAGIC
(1998)

Ain't no party like a witches' party, 'cause a witches' party don't stop. Even though it's twelve o'clock in the morning, sister witches Frances and Jet Owens are wide awake in the kitchen, reciting spells and whipping up frozen cocktails. The noisy blender awakens their nieces, Sally and Gillian, who hurry downstairs to join the late-night dance festivities. Now you can throw a midnight margarita bash of your own with these frosty flurries. Blended with your favorite tequila and orange liqueur—plus lime and coconut, just like the lyrics in the Harry Nilsson song featured in the movie—these magical margaritas will have you, too, grooving at midnight.

SERVES 4

1 cup (237 ml) silver or gold tequila
1 cup (237 ml) freshly squeezed lime juice (8 to 10 limes)
¾ cup (177 ml) cream of coconut (see Note)
½ cup (118 ml) orange liqueur, such as Triple Sec or Cointreau
6 cups (1420 ml) ice
Lime slices, for garnish
Fresh mint leaves, for garnish

In a blender, combine the tequila, lime juice, cream of coconut, orange liqueur, and ice. Blend until smooth, then pour into serving glasses and garnish with lime slices and mint leaves. Bone Appetit!

NOTE

Cream of coconut is a sweetened syrup sold in bottles for cocktail use. Do not substitute canned coconut cream, which is thicker and unsweetened.

“Flip the switch and let the cauldron bubble!”

—THE OWENS SISTERS

"Come and play with us, Danny. Forever . . . and ever . . . and ever."

—THE GRADY TWINS

REDRUM SANGRIA

THE SHINING
(1980)

The Torrance family is throwing a party in Room 237, and you're invited! Take a leisurely drive through the majestic Rocky Mountains, surrounded by towering pine trees and crystal clear rivers that sparkle in the sunlight. At the end of your journey, you'll be greeted by the expansive Overlook Hotel, a charming resort with mountain lodge aesthetics and a warm, welcoming staff. Jack and Wendy, your gracious hosts, will be serving their legendary Redrum Sangria, a refreshing beverage that's simply to die for. Made with Spanish red wine, orange and lemon juice, silver rum, and club soda, this luminous libation has a deep bloody hue and is terrifyingly tangy. Sangria, which translates to "bloodletting" in Spanish, is a classic cocktail prepared countless ways, but the famed Torrance family recipe will have you screaming with delight.

SERVES 6 TO 8

- 2 bottles (750 ml each) Spanish red wine, such as Rioja or Tempranillo
- ¾ cup (177 ml) freshly squeezed orange juice (2 to 3 oranges)
- ½ cup (99 g) granulated sugar
- 6 tablespoons (89 ml) freshly squeezed lemon juice (2 to 3 lemons)
- ¼ cup (59 ml) silver rum
- 1 cup plus 2 tablespoons (296 ml) club soda
- Orange, lemon, and lime slices, for garnish
- Ice, for serving

1 In a large pitcher, combine the wine, orange juice, sugar, lemon juice, and rum. Stir until the sugar dissolves, then cover the pitcher and refrigerate for 2 to 3 hours, until chilled. Keep refrigerated until ready to serve, or up to 3 days.

2 When ready to serve, add the club soda and stir to combine, then add several citrus slices to the pitcher. Place a few ice cubes and citrus slices into each glass, then pour the sangria and serve. Bone Appetit!

LADIES' NIGHT PITCHER MARTINIS

THE WITCHES OF EASTWICK (1987)

Longtime friends Alex, Jane, and Sukie are a trio of witches—but they don't realize it yet. On a rainy Thursday evening, they meet at Alex's house for their weekly ladies' night, complete with popcorn, crackers, spray cheese, and a tall pitcher of martinis. While commiserating about their lackluster love lives over cocktails and snacks, their combined powers unknowingly manifest the man of their dreams. Pick a date, invite your coven, and conjure a night to remember with these potent pitcher martinis. Served with an array of enchanted garnishes, this entertaining build-your-own martini station ensures everyone can summon the drink their heart desires.

1 bottle (750 ml) gin or vodka
2½ ounces (74 ml) dry vermouth
Ice, for shaking and serving

GARNISH SUGGESTIONS

Lemon peel twist
Lime peel twist
Orange peel twist
Cocktail onions
Pimento-stuffed olives
Blue-cheese-stuffed olives
Garlic-stuffed olives
Cornichon pickles
Cucumber slices
Fresh rosemary sprigs
Fresh thyme sprigs
Fresh mint sprigs

1 In a pitcher, combine the gin and vermouth. Refrigerate for 3 to 4 hours, until chilled, and keep refrigerated until ready to serve.

2 Place the garnishes of your choice into separate bowls, allowing guests to customize their drinks.

3 There are three ways to prepare the martinis: shaken, stirred, and on the rocks.

4 To make a shaken martini, pour 3 ounces of the martini mix into a cocktail shaker. Fill with ice, shake vigorously for 20 seconds, then strain into a martini or coupe glass.

5 To make a stirred martini, pour 3 ounces of the martini mix into a large glass. Add several ice cubes and stir in a circular motion for 20 seconds, then strain into a martini or coupe glass.

6 To serve a martini on the rocks, pour 3 ounces of the martini mix into a rocks or old-fashioned glass, then add a few ice cubes and serve. This method is less traditional, but it's the quickest way to serve a large crowd.

"I really like our Thursday nights. It's the only time I get to, you know, really relax."

—JANE SPOFFORD

MY REPLY
IS
NO
1862DP

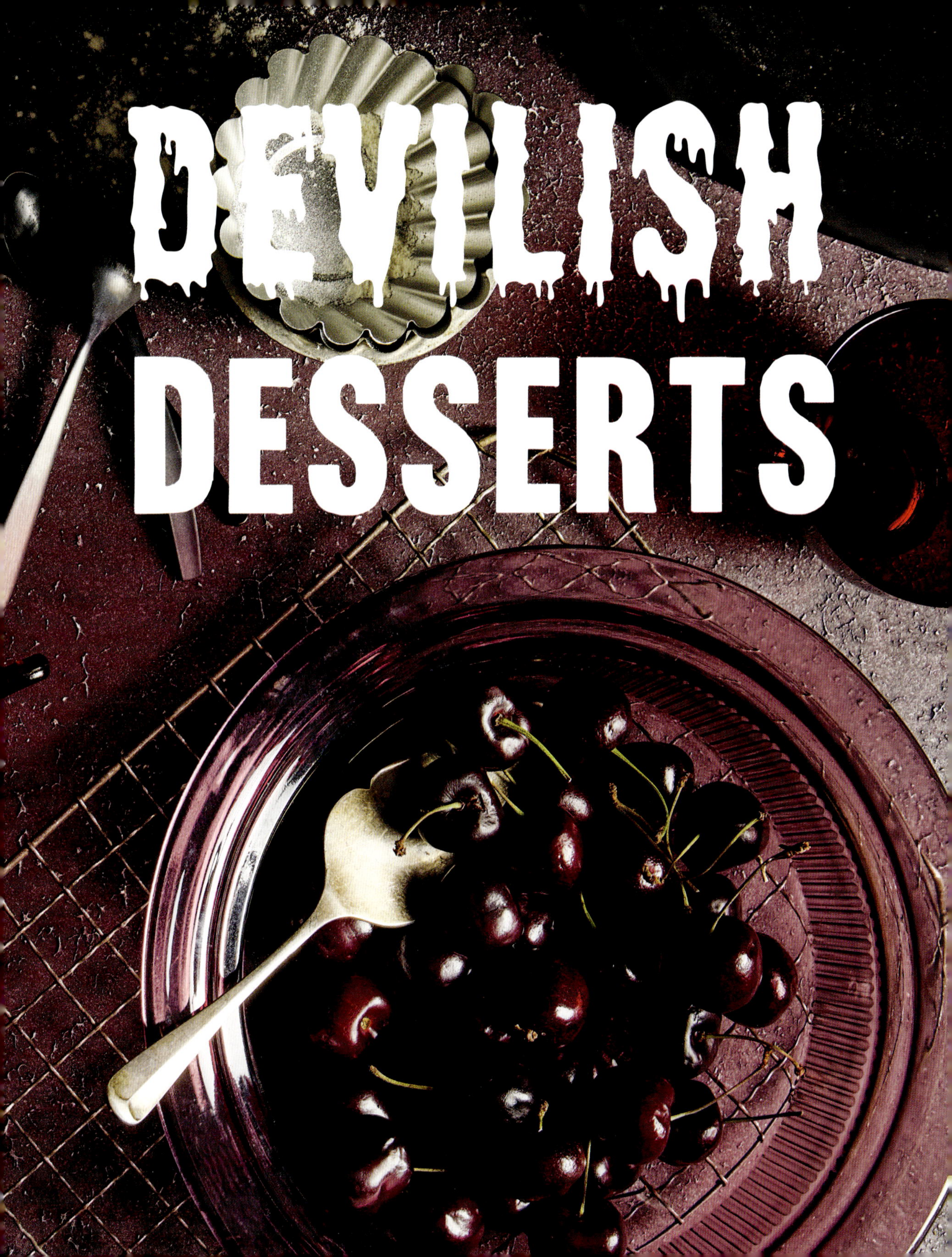
DEVILISH
DESSERTS

THE FOLLOWING PAGES CONTAIN TEMPTING CONTENT. VIEWER DISCRETION IS ADVISED.

If you're sensitive to chocolate, caramel, marshmallows, and whipped cream, please proceed with caution. Don't be surprised if you spontaneously start dancing after trying Tally Me Banana Cupcakes (page 149) in tribute to **BEETLEJUICE**. Be prepared to teleport to another world with **CORALINE**'s chocolate Black Button Cookies (page 159). And if you ain't afraid of no ghosts, That's a Big Twinkie Cake (page 167), inspired by the classic line in **GHOSTBUSTERS**, will fulfill all your childhood dreams. Sinful, decadent, and delicious, there are seventeen Devilish Desserts in this chapter that'll capture your soul forever.

"Come, mister tally man,
tally me banana . . ."
—HARRY BELAFONTE VIA DELIA DEETZ

TALLY ME BANANA CUPCAKES

BEETLEJUICE

(1988)

Delia Deetz's networking party is off to a rough start. Her guests are bored and uninterested, and the crickets chirping outside are louder than the awkward conversation flailing around the dinner table. When the Maitlands—a married ghost couple living in the attic—attempt to terrify the mortals by possessing their bodies to dance and sing along to "Day-O" by Harry Belafonte, their plan backfires after the victims unexpectedly enjoy the experience and the party is resurrected. In tribute to the lyrics of this iconic song, these captivating cupcakes are baked with warm spices and a beautiful bunch of ripe bananas. Topped with a silky-smooth vanilla frosting and sprinkled with a pinch of cinnamon—daylight come and me wan' go home.

MAKES 22 TO 24 CUPCAKES

FOR THE CUPCAKES

- 2 cups (240 g) all-purpose flour
- 1 teaspoon baking powder
- 1 teaspoon baking soda
- ¾ teaspoon salt
- ½ teaspoon ground cinnamon
- ⅛ teaspoon ground nutmeg
- 12 tablespoons (1½ sticks/170 g) unsalted butter, at room temperature
- 1½ cups (297 g) granulated sugar
- 3 large eggs, at room temperature
- 2 teaspoons vanilla extract
- 1¾ cups (420 g) mashed bananas (4 to 5 medium bananas, see Note)
- ½ cup (114 g) sour cream, at room temperature

FOR THE FROSTING

- 1½ cups (3 sticks/341 g) unsalted butter, at room temperature
- 4½ cups (511 g) powdered sugar
- 1½ tablespoons vanilla extract
- ¾ teaspoon salt
- Ground cinnamon, for garnish

1. Preheat the oven to 350°F (177°C) and fill two 12-cup cupcake pans with paper liners.

2. **MAKE THE CUPCAKES:** In a medium bowl, whisk together the flour, baking powder, baking soda, salt, cinnamon, and nutmeg. Set aside.

3. In a large mixing bowl, using an electric mixer, beat the butter and granulated sugar on medium speed until light and fluffy. Add the eggs and vanilla and beat until smooth. Add the bananas and beat until evenly combined. Add approximately one-third of the flour mixture and beat until no dry streaks remain, then add half of the sour cream and beat to combine. Add another third of the flour mixture, and beat to combine, then add the remaining sour cream and beat to combine. Add the remaining flour mixture and beat until no dry streaks remain.

4. Evenly divide the batter among the prepared cupcake pans, filling each one about three-quarters full. Bake for 18 to 22 minutes, until a toothpick inserted into the center of a

recipe continues

cupcake comes out clean with a few moist crumbs sticking to it. Let the cupcakes cool in the pans for 5 minutes, then transfer to a wire rack to cool completely, 30 to 45 minutes.

5 **MAKE THE FROSTING:** In a large mixing bowl, using an electric mixer, beat the butter on medium speed until smooth, then sift in the powdered sugar. Beat on medium speed until light and fluffy, then add the vanilla and salt and beat until smooth.

6 To decorate the cupcakes, transfer the frosting to a piping bag or a zip-top bag with a corner cut off and decorate each cupcake with a generous swirl of frosting. Garnish each cupcake with a pinch of cinnamon. Bone Appetit!

NOTE

When selecting ripe bananas, look for fruit that is yellow with little brown freckles, not covered in dark brown patches.

CHUCKY-LATE CHOCOLATE CHIP CAKE

CHILD'S PLAY
(1988)

Be careful what you wish for. Andy Barclay gets exactly what he wants on his sixth birthday: a talking Good Guy doll named Chucky, who instantly becomes his new best friend. That evening, while Andy's mother is working late at the department store, Chucky comes alive and viciously murders the babysitter. Fortunately, she manages to enjoy a few bites of Andy's homemade birthday cake before her untimely demise. Ultra-rich and fudgy, this triple chocolate cake is studded with chocolate chips and covered in a silky-smooth chocolate frosting. This simple, one-bowl recipe is so easy to make, it's practically child's play.

MAKES 1 NINE-INCH DOUBLE-LAYER CAKE

FOR THE CAKE

- Softened butter for greasing the pans
- 1 cup (170 g) semisweet chocolate chips
- 3 cups plus 1 tablespoon (368 g) all-purpose flour, divided
- 2 cups (396 g) granulated sugar
- ½ cup plus 2 tablespoons (54 g) unsweetened cocoa powder (see Note)
- 2 teaspoons baking soda
- 1 teaspoon salt
- 2 cups (473 ml) water
- ¾ cup (177 ml) vegetable oil
- ¼ cup (59 ml) distilled white vinegar
- 2 teaspoons vanilla extract

FOR THE CHOCOLATE FROSTING

- 18 tablespoons (2¼ sticks/257 g) unsalted butter, at room temperature
- 3 cups (341 g) powdered sugar
- ¾ cup (63 g) unsweetened cocoa powder
- 2 teaspoons vanilla extract
- ½ teaspoon salt

FOR THE COLORED FROSTING (OPTIONAL)

- 8 tablespoons (1 stick/113 g) unsalted butter, at room temperature
- 1½ cups (170 g) powdered sugar
- 1 teaspoon vanilla extract
- ¼ teaspoon salt
- Food dye, any colors you like

1 Preheat the oven to 350°F (177°C). Grease the bottom and sides of two 9-inch round cake pans with butter, then line the bottom of the pans with a circle of parchment paper.

2 **MAKE THE CAKE:** In a small bowl, combine the chocolate chips and 1 tablespoon of the flour. Toss to evenly coat the chips with the flour. Set aside.

3 Over a large mixing bowl, place a wire mesh strainer with the remaining 3 cups of flour, the granulated sugar, cocoa powder, baking soda, and salt. Sift the dry ingredients into the bowl, then whisk together until evenly combined. Add the water, oil, vinegar, and vanilla, then stir until smooth and blended. Add the chocolate chips and any remaining flour in the bowl, then stir using a silicone spatula to combine.

recipe continues

4 Divide the batter evenly between the two prepared cake pans, then bake for 30 to 35 minutes, until a toothpick inserted into the center of the cake comes out clean with a few moist crumbs sticking to it. Let the cakes cool in the pans for 5 minutes, then invert onto a wire rack. Peel off the parchment paper and let cool to room temperature, 45 to 60 minutes. Wrap the cakes tightly in plastic and refrigerate until chilled, at least 4 hours or up to 2 days.

5 **MAKE THE CHOCOLATE FROSTING:** In a large mixing bowl, using an electric mixer, beat the butter on medium speed until smooth. Place a wire-mesh strainer over the bowl and sift in the powdered sugar and cocoa powder. Beat on medium speed until light and fluffy, then add the vanilla and salt and beat until smooth.

6 **MAKE THE COLORED FROSTING (IF DESIRED):** In a medium bowl, using an electric mixer, beat the butter on medium speed until smooth. Place a wire-mesh strainer over the bowl and sift in the powdered sugar. Beat on medium speed until light and fluffy, then add the vanilla and salt and beat until smooth. Use food dye to tint the frosting—if using more than one color, divide the frosting into separate bowls and tint each one individually.

7 **DECORATE THE CAKE:** Unwrap one of the chilled cake layers and place it on a serving plate. Scoop about ¾ cup of the chocolate frosting on top of the cake and spread it into an even layer. Place the second cake layer on top and use the remaining frosting to evenly coat the top and sides of the cake.

8 If using colored frosting, transfer it to piping bags and pipe the design of your choice on the cake. Bone Appetit!

NOTE

Cocoa powder is available in two common types: natural cocoa and Dutch-process cocoa. Natural cocoa is reddish-brown, while Dutch-process cocoa is almost black. Either kind will work for this recipe.

"Hi, I'm Chucky. Wanna play?"

—CHUCKY

APPLE CIDER CHURROS WITH DULCE DE LECHE

On Día de los Muertos, Mexican families honor their deceased loved ones by creating an ofrenda, an elaborate home altar decorated with bright marigolds, glowing candles, and their favorite foods they once enjoyed. In *Coco*, the spirits get to bring those treats back to the Land of the Dead when the holiday is over—if they can clear them through customs. Skeletal travelers arrive at the security checkpoint, carrying their families' offerings: from bottles of wine and fresh fruit to pan de muerto and homemade churros. Enter these golden apple cider churros—crisp on the outside and tender within, they're baked with fresh apple juice, cinnamon, nutmeg, and vanilla. Rolled in cinnamon-sugar and served with a rich dulce de leche dipping sauce, these heavenly treats are little bites of love.

COCO
(2017)

MAKES 25 TO 30 CHURROS

FOR THE DULCE DE LECHE

1 (14-ounce/397 g) can sweetened condensed milk

FOR THE CHURROS

1 cup (120 g) all-purpose flour
1 teaspoon ground cinnamon
¼ teaspoon ground nutmeg
¼ teaspoon ground allspice
¼ teaspoon salt
¾ cup plus 3 tablespoons (222 ml) unfiltered apple juice
8 tablespoons (1 stick/113 g) unsalted butter
2 tablespoons dark brown sugar
1 tablespoon freshly squeezed lemon juice
2 large eggs, at room temperature
1 teaspoon vanilla extract
1½ quarts (1.4 L) vegetable oil, if frying

FOR THE TOPPING

½ cup (99 g) granulated sugar
1 tablespoon ground cinnamon
⅛ teaspoon salt
4 tablespoons (½ stick/57 g) unsalted butter, melted, if baking

1. **MAKE THE DULCE DE LECHE (SEE NOTES):** Remove the label from the can of condensed milk, then place the entire unopened can on its side in a large, deep pot. Note: placing the can on its side prevents it from banging around in the pot once the water is at a rolling boil. Fill the pot with water so the surface of the water is several inches above the can. Cover the pot, set over high heat, and bring to a boil. Then reduce the heat and simmer gently for 3 hours, periodically lifting the lid to make sure the water line stays at least 2 inches above the can, and adding more boiling water, if needed, to keep the can fully submerged for important safety reasons (see Notes).

2. Use tongs to remove the hot can from the water and place it on a wire rack to fully cool to room temperature. For safety reasons, do not attempt to open the can while it is hot.

3. **MAKE THE CHURROS:** Prepare a piping bag with a wide star tip. Set aside.

4. In a small bowl, whisk together the flour, cinnamon, nutmeg, allspice, and salt. Set aside.

recipe continues

5 In a small saucepan, combine the apple juice, butter, brown sugar, and lemon juice. Place over medium heat and stir until the butter melts. As soon as the mixture begins to boil, add all the flour mixture at once and stir vigorously until the dough forms a ball that pulls away from the sides of the pan, about 1 minute. Remove from the heat and transfer the dough to a large mixing bowl. Use an electric mixer to beat the dough until it is warm but no longer hot to the touch. With the mixer running, add the eggs one at a time, beating until blended between each addition. Add the vanilla and continue beating for 2 to 3 minutes, until smooth and glossy. The dough will still be slightly warm. Transfer the dough to the prepared piping bag.

6 **MAKE THE TOPPING:** In a small, wide bowl, stir together the granulated sugar, cinnamon, and salt. If baking the churros, have the melted butter ready.

OPTION 1: Fry the Churros

1 If frying the churros, pour the vegetable oil into a large, deep saucepan or wide skillet and set over medium-high heat until the oil temperature reaches 360° to 365°F (182° to 185°C) on a deep-fry thermometer. Cover a heatproof plate with several layers of paper towels and place it near the pan of oil.

2 Pipe 3-inch lines of dough directly into the hot oil, using scissors to cut them off cleanly. Cook for 1 to 2 minutes, until golden brown on the bottom, then flip and repeat on the second side. Transfer the churros to the prepared plate to drain for about 1 minute. Toss the hot churros in the bowl of cinnamon-sugar until evenly coated, then transfer to a wire rack. Repeat with the remaining dough, adjusting the heat as needed so the oil stays at the correct temperature. Only cook 3 to 4 churros at a time, since crowding the pan with too many churros can cause the oil temperature to drop.

OPTION 2: Bake the Churros

1 If baking the churros, preheat the oven to 350°F (177°C) and line a baking sheet with parchment paper.

2 Pipe a 3-inch line of dough onto the prepared baking sheet, using scissors to cut it off cleanly. Repeat with the remaining dough, leaving ½ inch of space between each churro, since they do not spread while baking. Bake for 20 minutes, then flip the churros over and continue baking for 20 to 25 minutes, until deeply golden brown. Note: if they look pale or just lightly golden, they are not done yet.

3 When the churros are finished baking, remove the baking sheet from the oven. Immediately, brush one of the churros with melted butter, covering all sides, then dip it in the bowl of cinnamon-sugar until evenly coated. Place on a wire rack, then repeat with the remaining churros.

4 When ready to serve, transfer the dulce de leche to a small bowl and warm it briefly in the microwave until it reaches a thin, dippable texture.

5 Serve the churros warm, with warm dulce de leche for dipping. Bone Appetit!

NOTES

When boiling the can of condensed milk, it is absolutely vital that the water level stays several inches above the can at all times. If the water in the pan evaporates, the pressure inside the can may cause it to explode.

Instead of making homemade dulce de leche, you could simply buy a can of prepared dulce de leche, commonly found in the Latin section of many grocery stores.

"Some churros, from my family."

—DECEASED TRAVELER

"Black is traditional. But if you'd prefer pink, or vermilion, or chartreuse . . ."
—THE OTHER MOTHER

BLACK BUTTON COOKIES

CORALINE
(2009)

These cute-as-a-button treats might not be Cocoa Beetles from Zanzibar, but they'll be the first thing to disappear at your next Halloween party. Inspired by the Other Mother's shiny black button eyes, these crafty cookies taste just like classic Oreos. Two extra-crispy, extra-chocolatey discs are sandwiched together with smooth vanilla filling. Your first bite will take you through a portal to a parallel world—just don't forget to lock the door when you come back.

MAKES 18 TO 20 SANDWICH COOKIES

FOR THE COOKIES

- 1¾ cups (210 g) all-purpose flour
- 1 cup (84 g) unsweetened Dutch-process cocoa powder (see Note)
- 1 teaspoon salt
- ¼ teaspoon baking soda
- 16 tablespoons (2 sticks/227 g) unsalted butter, at room temperature
- 1 cup (198 g) granulated sugar
- 1 large egg, at room temperature
- 1 teaspoon vanilla extract

FOR THE FILLING

- 8 tablespoons (1 stick/113 g) unsalted butter, at room temperature
- 2 cups (227 g) powdered sugar
- 2 teaspoons vanilla extract
- ¼ teaspoon salt

1 **MAKE THE COOKIES:** Over a medium bowl, place a wire-mesh strainer with the flour, cocoa powder, salt, and baking soda. Sift the dry ingredients into the bowl, then set aside.

2 In a large mixing bowl, using an electric mixer, beat the butter and granulated sugar on medium speed until blended. Add the egg and vanilla and beat until smooth. Add the flour mixture and beat until no dry streaks remain. Gather the dough, then divide in half. Roll each half into a ball, wrap tightly in plastic, then flatten slightly to make a disc shape and refrigerate for at least 2 hours. The dough can keep in the fridge for up to 1 week.

3 To bake the cookies, preheat the oven to 350°F (177°C) and line two or more baking sheets with parchment paper.

4 Remove the discs of dough from the fridge and allow to rest at room temperature for 30 minutes to soften. Unwrap one of the discs of dough and place it on a large square of parchment paper. Place another square of parchment on top of the dough and use a rolling pin to flatten the dough between the two pieces of parchment until it makes a large circle approximately ¼ inch thick. Remove the top sheet of parchment and use a 2-inch circle cutter to cut out circles of dough. Transfer the circles to the prepared baking sheets, leaving about 1 inch of space between each cookie, and placing 12 to 15 cookies per sheet. Gather and reroll the dough scraps, then cut out the remaining cookies. Repeat with the second disc of dough.

recipe continues

5 To make the button design, select a smaller circle cutter, approximately 1¾ inches. Turn the cutter over and use the dull, rounded side (not the sharp side) to gently press into one of the cookies, creating a shallow indentation without cutting all the way through. Then, use a drinking straw to cut out four holes in the center of each cookie. Repeat with the other cookies. Place the baking sheets in the freezer for 15 minutes; this helps the cookies keep their shape while baking.

6 Transfer the baking sheets directly to the oven and bake for 8 to 10 minutes. If baking two pans at once, swap the positions of the pans halfway through to ensure the cookies bake evenly. Let the cookies cool on the baking sheets for 5 minutes, then transfer to a wire rack to cool completely.

7 **MAKE THE FILLING:** In a large mixing bowl, using an electric mixer, beat the butter on medium speed until smooth, then sift in the powdered sugar. Beat on low speed to combine, then raise the speed to medium and continue beating until blended. Add the vanilla and salt and beat until light and fluffy.

8 **ASSEMBLE THE COOKIES:** Arrange half of the cookies with the flat side up. Spread about 2 teaspoons of filling over each cookie, then place a second cookie on top to make a sandwich. Repeat with the remaining cookies and filling. Bone Appetit!

NOTE

Unsweetened cocoa is available in two common types: natural cocoa (which has a reddish-brown color) and Dutch-process (which is almost black).
Be sure to use Dutch-process in this recipe for best results.

MOLTEN RED CHOCOLATE DEMON CAKES

THE EVIL DEAD
(1981)

Ash Williams and his four friends hoped their weekend getaway at a rustic cabin would be relaxing, but things didn't go exactly as planned. They accidentally unleash a demonic curse, Ash's friends are brutally murdered one by one, and their corpses return to life as bloodthirsty Deadites, savagely attacking everyone in sight. Thankfully, once Ash throws the Book of the Dead into a burning fireplace, the evil curse is lifted, and the Deadites decompose into steaming puddles of guts and bubbling slime. Dedicated to the bloody creatures in this classic film, these individual-size demon cakes ooze with molten red chocolate, hidden within the center of a rich, gooey, and intensely chocolatey cake. One bite and you'll be possessed to try more.

MAKES 5 INDIVIDUAL-SIZE CAKES

FOR THE MOLTEN CENTERS

1 cup (150 g) red candy melts

1½ tablespoons vegetable shortening

¼ teaspoon unsweetened Dutch-process cocoa powder (see Note)

Pinch of salt

5 paper mini cupcake liners

FOR THE CAKES

1 to 2 teaspoons unsweetened cocoa powder, for dusting the ramekins

8 tablespoons (1 stick/113 g) unsalted butter, plus more for greasing the ramekins

½ cup (85 g) semisweet chocolate (50 to 60% cacao), chopped or chips

½ cup (85 g) bittersweet chocolate (70 to 80% cacao), chopped or chips

1 teaspoon vanilla extract

¼ cup (30 g) all-purpose flour

½ cup (57 g) powdered sugar

¼ teaspoon salt

2 large eggs, at room temperature

2 large egg yolks, at room temperature

1 **MAKE THE MOLTEN CENTERS:** Place the candy melts into a heatproof bowl and melt in the microwave according to the package directions. Once melted, add the vegetable shortening, cocoa powder, and a pinch of salt and stir until blended. Pour about 1½ tablespoons of the mixture into each mini cupcake liner, filling the liners about three-quarters full. Transfer to the fridge for 15 to 20 minutes to solidify, then keep at room temperature for up to 1 hour, until ready to use.

2 Preheat the oven to 425°F (218°C). Grease five ramekins with butter. Place a spoonful of cocoa powder in one of the ramekins and tilt it around until the sides and bottom are evenly coated in a layer of cocoa. Pour the excess cocoa into the next ramekin and repeat until all of them have been dusted in cocoa, tapping the ramekins to discard any excess.

3 **MAKE THE CAKES:** Fill a small saucepan with 1 to 2 inches of water and bring to a simmer over medium heat. Place a small heatproof bowl over the pan, so the bottom of the bowl rests above the surface of the simmering water, but not touching. Place the butter, semisweet chocolate, and

recipe continues

bittersweet chocolate into the bowl and stir until melted and smooth with no lumps remaining. Carefully remove the hot bowl from the pan and stir in the vanilla. Set aside to cool for 5 to 10 minutes.

4 In a small bowl, whisk together the flour, sugar, and salt. Set aside.

5 In a large mixing bowl, using an electric mixer, beat the eggs and egg yolks on medium-high speed for 4 to 6 minutes, until thick and foamy. Add the flour mixture and stir by hand, using a silicone spatula, until no dry streaks remain. Add the melted chocolate and stir, again by hand, until smooth and blended with no streaks remaining.

6 Pour ¼ cup of the batter into each prepared ramekin, then place a molten center in the middle of each one. Divide the remaining batter evenly among the ramekins. There should be about ½ inch of space at the top of each one, so do not overfill. Place the ramekins on a rimmed baking sheet and bake for 13 to 16 minutes, until the edges are set and dry and the centers still look soft.

7 Let the cakes cool in the ramekins for 1 minute, then invert onto serving plates and serve immediately while hot. Bone Appetit!

NOTE

Unsweetened cocoa is available in two common types: natural cocoa (which has a reddish-brown color) and Dutch-process (which is almost black). Be sure to use Dutch-process in this recipe for best results.

"Join us."
—DEADITES

"You should learn not
to compete with me.
I always win!"
—MADELINE ASHTON

MADELINE'S MADELEINES

Keep your friends close and your frenemies closer. Aging Broadway diva Madeline Ashton is consumed by vanity and driven by jealousy, and obsessed with outshining and destroying her lifelong rival, Helen Sharp. She steals Helen's handsome fiancé and marries him, then later shoots Helen in the stomach with a shotgun. Youth and beauty may be fleeting, but these golden madeleines named after Madeline are eternal. Flavored with vanilla and freshly grated lemon zest, then finished with a dusting of powdered sugar, be warned: these soft and tender, lemony French sponge cakes are highly addictive. *"Now a warning?!"*

DEATH BECOMES HER
(1992)

MAKES ABOUT 20 MADELEINES

1 cup (120 g) all-purpose flour
½ teaspoon baking powder
¼ teaspoon salt
2 large eggs, at room temperature
⅔ cup (132 g) granulated sugar
2 tablespoons powdered sugar, plus more for dusting (optional)
Grated zest from 2 lemons
1 teaspoon vanilla extract
8 tablespoons (1 stick/113 g) unsalted butter, melted, plus more softened for greasing the pans

1 In a small bowl, whisk together the flour, baking powder, and salt. Set aside.

2 In a large mixing bowl, using an electric mixer, beat the eggs on medium-high speed for 2 to 3 minutes, until thick and foamy. With the mixer running, slowly add the granulated sugar, followed by the powdered sugar. Add the zest and vanilla, then continue to beat for 3 to 4 minutes, until the mixture forms smooth ribbons when the beaters are lifted. Add the flour mixture and stir gently by hand, using a silicone spatula, until no dry streaks remain. Add the butter and stir gently until the mixture is smooth and blended, without overmixing. Transfer the dough to a smaller bowl, then cover with plastic and place in the fridge for at least 60 minutes or preferably overnight.

3 Preheat the oven to 375°F (191°C). Grease two madeleine pans with butter, then place them in the freezer to chill for at least 10 minutes.

4 Remove the chilled pans from the freezer and place 1 heaping tablespoon of dough into the center of each well. Note: do not spread the dough, as it will spread in the pan while it bakes. If baking only one pan at a time, keep the remaining dough in the fridge until ready to bake.

5 Bake for 9 to 11 minutes, until the edges are golden and the tops of the cookies spring back when lightly pressed. Cool in the pan for 5 minutes, then transfer to a wire rack to cool. Just before serving, lightly dust the cookies with powdered sugar, if desired. Bone Appetit!

NOTE

Madeleines are best on the day they are baked, as they quickly lose their delicate texture.

"That's a big Twinkie."

—WINSTON ZEDDEMORE

THAT'S A BIG TWINKIE CAKE

Paranormal psychokinetic energy is surging in New York City. Ghost sightings are skyrocketing, and the Ghostbusters—Ray, Egon, Peter, and Winston—are so busy that their ghost storage tank is nearly at capacity. To help everyone understand the magnitude of the situation, Egon compares the increase in supernatural energy to a Hostess Twinkie that's "35 feet long, weighing approximately 600 pounds." Sure, this cake isn't quite that big, but at least it'll fit in your oven! Light and moist like the original treats, this enlarged golden replica also features a silky vanilla-cream center. The next time you're craving those soft sponge cake snacks from your childhood . . . who you gonna call? This cookbook.

MAKES ONE 10-INCH RING CAKE

FOR THE CAKE

- 16 tablespoons (2 sticks/227 g) unsalted butter, at room temperature, plus more for greasing the pan
- 2½ cups (300 g) cake flour, plus more for dusting the pan
- ¼ cup (30 g) cornstarch
- 2½ teaspoons baking powder
- 1½ teaspoons salt
- 2 cups (396 g) granulated sugar
- 6 large eggs, yolks and whites separated, at room temperature
- 1½ tablespoons vanilla extract
- 1 cup (237 ml) whole milk, at room temperature, divided

FOR THE FILLING

- 1 (7-ounce/198 g) jar Jet-Puffed marshmallow crème (see Note)
- 8 tablespoons (1 stick/113 g) unsalted butter, at room temperature
- 2 tablespoons powdered sugar
- 2 teaspoons vanilla extract
- ⅛ teaspoon salt

1 Preheat the oven to 325°F (163°C). Grease a 10-inch bundt cake pan with decorative ridges with butter, then add a spoonful of cake flour and tilt it around until the sides and bottom are evenly coated in a layer of flour. Tap the pan to discard the excess flour and set aside.

2 **MAKE THE CAKE:** In a medium bowl, whisk together the cake flour, cornstarch, baking powder, and salt. Set aside.

3 In a large mixing bowl, using an electric mixer, beat the butter and granulated sugar until light and fluffy. With the mixer running, add the egg yolks one at a time, beating until smooth after each addition. Add the vanilla and beat until blended. Add approximately one-third of the flour mixture and beat until no dry streaks remain, then add ½ cup of the milk and beat to combine. Add another third of the flour mixture and beat to combine, then add the remaining milk and beat to combine. Add the remaining flour mixture and beat until no dry streaks remain.

4 In a large, clean mixing bowl, using an electric mixer, beat the egg whites on medium-high speed for 3 to 4 minutes, until firm peaks form when the beaters

recipe continues

are lifted. Add the egg whites to the batter and using a silicone spatula, gently fold in the egg whites until no streaks remain; do not over-stir or the batter will deflate. Pour the batter into the prepared cake pan, spreading it into an even layer.

5 Bake for 50 to 60 minutes, until a toothpick or paring knife inserted deep into the center of the cake comes out clean with a few moist crumbs sticking to it. Cool in the pan for 10 minutes, then invert onto a wire rack to cool completely for 1½ to 2 hours.

6 **MAKE THE FILLING:** In a large mixing bowl, using an electric mixer, beat the marshmallow crème and butter on medium-high speed until light and fluffy. Sift in the powdered sugar, then add the vanilla and salt and beat until smooth. Transfer to a piping bag or a zip-top bag with the corner cut off.

7 Once the cake is completely cool, flip it over so the bottom faces up. Use a paring knife or apple corer to cut a series of 1-inch holes evenly spaced around the bottom of the cake—each hole should be about 1 inch apart and approximately 1½ inches deep. Use a knife or your fingers to carve out tunnels between each hole, creating a hollow space inside the cake. Feel free to save the scooped-out bits for snacking.

8 Insert the tip of the piping bag into the holes and fill them evenly, creating a ring of filling inside the cake. Carefully flip the cake onto a platter and serve. Bone Appetit!

NOTE

Be sure to use Jet-Puffed marshmallow crème, since using other brands like Marshmallow Fluff can result in a runny filling.

S'MORES CUPCAKES WITH TOASTED MARSHMALLOW

The Ghostbusters are New York City's only hope to stop the Stay-Puft Marshmallow Man from destroying Manhattan. Made entirely of marshmallow and standing over one hundred feet tall, this gigantic confectionery beast is on a rampage, crushing cars and causing panic in the streets. In a desperate last measure, the Ghostbusters fire their proton pack guns at the creature, intentionally crossing the energy streams to trigger a massive explosion that obliterates Mr. Stay-Puft, coating the entire block in a thick, gooey layer of toasted marshmallow. In celebration of the demon's demise, these scrumptious s'mores cupcakes are marshmallow-marvelous! King-size chunks of Hershey's milk chocolate bars are nestled inside a soft graham cracker cupcake. Topped with a generous swirl of homemade marshmallow that's toasted until golden and melty, you can now enjoy your favorite campfire treats in the form of a cute cupcake!

MAKES 18 TO 20 CUPCAKES

FOR THE CUPCAKES

- 1¼ cups (130 g) graham cracker crumbs (about 9 crackers)
- 1 cup (120 g) all-purpose flour
- 1 teaspoon baking powder
- ¾ teaspoon baking soda
- ½ teaspoon salt
- ½ cup (118 ml) whole milk, at room temperature
- ½ cup (114 g) sour cream, at room temperature
- 12 tablespoons (1½ sticks/170 g) unsalted butter, at room temperature
- ½ cup (107 g) packed dark brown sugar
- ½ cup (99 g) granulated sugar
- 2 large eggs, at room temperature
- 2 teaspoons vanilla extract
- 1½ cups (210 g) chopped Hershey's milk chocolate bars (about 5 bars)

FOR THE TOASTED MARSHMALLOW

- 4 large egg whites
- 1½ cups (297 g) granulated sugar
- ½ cup (156 g) light corn syrup
- ½ teaspoon salt
- 2 teaspoons vanilla extract

1 Preheat the oven to 350°F (177°C) and fill two 12-cup cupcake pans with paper liners.

2 **MAKE THE CUPCAKES:** In a small bowl, whisk together the graham cracker crumbs, flour, baking powder, baking soda, and salt. Set aside.

3 In a small bowl or measuring cup, whisk together the milk and sour cream until blended. Set aside.

4 In a large mixing bowl, using an electric mixer, beat the butter, brown sugar, and granulated sugar on medium speed until light and fluffy. Add the eggs and vanilla and beat until smooth. Add approximately one-third of the flour mixture and beat until no dry streaks remain, then add half of the milk mixture and beat to combine. Add another third of the flour mixture and beat to combine, then add the remaining milk mixture and beat to combine. Add the remaining flour mixture and beat until no dry streaks remain. Add the chocolate and stir by hand, using a silicone spatula, until evenly distributed in the batter.

recipe continues

Guest Receipt
Date
Amount
Guests
Server
Total
MCO325-7

5 Pour the batter into the prepared cupcake pans, filling each one about three-quarters full. Bake for 18 to 22 minutes, until a toothpick inserted into the center of a cupcake comes out clean with a few moist crumbs sticking to it. Let the cupcakes cool in the pan for 5 minutes, then transfer to a wire rack to cool completely.

6 **MAKE THE TOASTED MARSHMALLOW:** Fill a small saucepan with 1 to 2 inches water and bring to a simmer over medium heat. Place a small heatproof bowl over the pan, so the bottom of the bowl rests above the surface of the simmering water; the bowl should not touch the water. Place the egg whites, granulated sugar, corn syrup, and salt into the bowl and whisk together until the sugar dissolves and the mixture reaches 140°F (60°C) on a cooking thermometer.

7 Carefully remove the hot bowl from the pan, then pour the mixture into a large mixing bowl. Using an electric mixer, beat on high speed until stiff peaks form when the beaters are lifted, about 5 minutes. Add the vanilla and beat until smooth and glossy.

8 Transfer the marshmallow mixture to a piping bag or a zip-top bag with the corner cut off, then pipe a generous swirl onto each cupcake. Use a kitchen torch to toast the marshmallow until golden. Bone Appetit!

"Funny, us going out like this. Killed by a hundred-foot marshmallow man."

—RAY STANTZ

MYERS'S MEYER LEMON BARS

HALLOWEEN

(1978)

Did you know that Michael Myers is an avid home baker? When he's not busy murdering innocent teenagers in Haddonfield, he enjoys spending time in the kitchen and surrounding himself with seasonal produce and fresh ingredients. Coming from a family of professional cooks, Michael showed an aptitude for knife skills at a young age. He even won first place at a local Halloween bake-off with these killer lemon bars. His buttery lemon crust slaughtered his competitors, and the luscious lemon filling was a cut above the rest. Dusted with a layer of powdered sugar, these award-winning treats seriously slay.

MAKES 28 TO 30 BARS

FOR THE CRUST

- 16 tablespoons (2 sticks/227 g) unsalted butter, at room temperature, plus more for greasing the baking dish
- ½ cup (99 g) granulated sugar
- ¼ cup (28 g) powdered sugar
- ½ teaspoon salt
- Grated zest from 2 lemons
- 2 cups (240 g) all-purpose flour

FOR THE FILLING

- 6 large eggs, at room temperature
- Grated zest from 2 lemons
- 1 cup (237 ml) freshly squeezed lemon juice (4 to 6 lemons)
- 1½ cups (297 g) granulated sugar
- ½ cup (57 g) powdered sugar, plus more for dusting the bars
- 6 tablespoons (45 g) all-purpose flour

1. Preheat the oven to 350°F (177°C). Grease a 9 x 13-inch baking dish with butter, then line it with a wide piece of parchment paper that covers the entire bottom of the dish and hangs over the sides by an inch or two. This creates a handle to easily lift the bars out later.

2. **MAKE THE CRUST:** In a large mixing bowl, using an electric mixer, beat the butter, granulated sugar, powdered sugar, salt, and lemon zest on medium speed until light and fluffy. Add the flour and beat until combined and sandy-textured. Press the mixture into the prepared baking dish, spreading it into an even layer. Using a fork, poke holes over the entire surface, then bake for 20 to 22 minutes, until lightly golden.

3. **MAKE THE FILLING:** In a medium bowl, whisk together the eggs, lemon zest, lemon juice, granulated sugar, powdered sugar, and flour until smooth and blended.

4. When the crust is finished baking, remove it from the oven and carefully pour the lemon filling mixture over the hot crust. Return the baking dish to the oven and bake for 20 to 25 minutes, until the center is set and no longer jiggles when the dish is nudged.

5. Place the dish on a wire rack to cool completely, for 60 minutes to 1¼ hours, then cover and refrigerate for 2 to 4 hours, until fully chilled and firm enough to slice.

6. When ready to serve, run a butter knife around the edges of the bars to loosen the sides, then use the parchment handles to lift the bars onto a cutting board. Cut into squares and dust them generously with powdered sugar just before serving. Bone Appetit!

"You can't kill
the boogeyman."
—TOMMY DOYLE

“Are you kids hungry? Does anybody want a cookie?”
—EMMA THE MAID

ATTIC COOKIES (CINNAMON SWIRL SNICKERDOODLES)

THE HAUNTED MANSION

(2003)

The Evers family's visit to Gracey Manor was meant to be a quick real-estate meeting, but when torrential rains flood the road, they're forced to spend the night. As siblings Michael and Megan wind down for the evening, a glowing blue orb appears in the bedroom. Curious, they follow it to a dark, dusty attic, where they're caught by the manor staff: Ezra, the grumpy footman, and Emma, the kind maid who offers them homemade cookies. Swirled with cinnamon and brown sugar, these spirited snickerdoodles are soft and chewy with a crackly top. Rolled in more cinnamon-sugar and baked until puffy and golden, this rapturous recipe will keep you happy "for Evers and Evers."

MAKES 24 TO 26 COOKIES

FOR THE CINNAMON SWIRL

½ cup (107 g) packed dark brown sugar
1 tablespoon ground cinnamon
⅛ teaspoon salt
4 tablespoons (½ stick/57 g) unsalted butter, at room temperature

FOR THE COOKIES

3 cups (360 g) all-purpose flour
1½ teaspoons cream of tartar
1 teaspoon baking soda
1 teaspoon salt
16 tablespoons (2 sticks/227 g) unsalted butter, at room temperature
1½ cups (297 g) granulated sugar
2 large eggs, at room temperature
2 teaspoons vanilla extract

FOR ROLLING

¼ cup (50 g) granulated sugar
1 teaspoon ground cinnamon
⅛ teaspoon salt

1 **MAKE THE CINNAMON SWIRL:** In a small bowl, stir together the brown sugar, cinnamon, and salt. Add the butter and stir until it forms a thick paste.

2 Place an 8-inch square of parchment or wax paper on a plate. Using your fingers, roll the cinnamon swirl paste into marble-size balls and place them on the parchment. Transfer the plate to the fridge to chill for 20 minutes.

3 **MAKE THE COOKIES:** In a medium bowl, whisk together the flour, cream of tartar, baking soda, and salt. Set aside.

4 In a large mixing bowl, using an electric mixer, beat the butter and granulated sugar on medium speed until light and fluffy. Add the eggs and vanilla and beat until smooth. Add the flour mixture and beat until no dry streaks remain. Using a silicone spatula, gradually add the chilled cinnamon swirl balls a few at a time, gently stirring between each addition, evenly distributing the balls throughout the dough—avoid overmixing to keep the cinnamon swirls intact. Transfer the dough to a smaller bowl, cover tightly with plastic, and refrigerate for at least 2 hours. The dough can keep in the fridge for up to 1 week.

5 To bake the cookies, preheat the oven to 350°F (177°C) and line two or more baking sheets with parchment paper.

6 In a small bowl, combine the granulated sugar, cinnamon, and salt.

recipe continues

7 Scoop the chilled dough into 2-tablespoon (40 g) balls, ensuring that the large cinnamon swirls are visible in each one. Roll the balls in the cinnamon-sugar mixture until evenly coated, then arrange on the prepared baking sheets, leaving 3 inches of space between each one and placing 6 cookies per baking sheet.

8 Bake for 11 to 13 minutes, until the edges are golden, the centers are set, and the cinnamon swirl appears melted and slightly caramelized. As soon as the cookies come out of the oven, use a spatula or round cookie cutter to gently nudge any misshapen cookies into circles. Let the cookies cool on the baking sheets for 10 minutes, then transfer to a wire rack to cool completely. Bone Appetit!

NEW ORLEANS BEIGNETS WITH RASPBERRY COULIS

Drinking blood for hundreds of years can start to feel monotonous. Sure, vital fluids are a crucial part of a vampire's diet, but it gets boring to only imbibe from human necks night after night. To switch things up, vampires will have an occasional cheat day and indulge in cruelty-free meals like Louis's Rat-atouille (page 97) and wash it down with a spicy, blood-free Lestat's Bloody Mary (page 124). Many vampires have a sweet fang, and those who live in New Orleans—like Louis and Lestat—will snack on beignets for dessert. Similar to doughnuts, these light, puffy pastries are fried until golden brown, then generously covered in powdered sugar. Served warm with a tangy raspberry coulis for dipping, these soft, pillowy squares are bloody delicious.

MAKES 32 TO 34 BEIGNETS

FOR THE RASPBERRY COULIS

- 3 cups (360 g) fresh or frozen raspberries
- ¼ cup (28 g) powdered sugar
- 4 teaspoons freshly squeezed lemon juice

FOR THE BEIGNETS

- ¾ cup (177 ml) whole milk
- ¼ cup (49 g) granulated sugar
- 2¼ teaspoons (1 packet) active dry yeast
- 3½ cups (420 g) all-purpose flour, plus more for dusting
- ½ teaspoon salt
- 1 large egg, at room temperature
- 3 tablespoons unsalted butter, at room temperature
- 1½ quarts (1.4 L) vegetable oil, for frying, plus more for greasing the bowl
- Powdered sugar, for dusting

1 **MAKE THE RASPBERRY COULIS:** Place the raspberries, powdered sugar, and lemon juice into a food processor or blender—if using frozen berries, defrost them first. Blend until smooth, then pour through a wire-mesh strainer to remove the seeds. Use immediately or cover and keep refrigerated until ready to serve, for up to 3 days. If desired, bring to room temperature before serving.

2 **MAKE THE BEIGNETS:** In a small saucepan, combine the milk, granulated sugar, and 2 tablespoons water. Stir to combine, then set the heat to medium-low and cook until the mixture reaches 110° to 115°F (43° to 46°C) on a cooking thermometer—it will feel warm to the touch, but not hot. Alternatively, you can heat the mixture in a heatproof bowl in the microwave until it reaches the correct temperature.

3 Pour the warm milk mixture into a large mixing bowl, then add the yeast and stir gently to combine. Let the mixture sit for 5 to 10 minutes, until the yeast becomes foamy. Add the flour and salt and stir until a dough begins to form. Add the egg, then the butter, 1 tablespoon at a time, stirring after each addition. Transfer the dough to a work surface and knead for 6 to 8 minutes, until glossy and stretchy. Note that this dough is wet and sticky at first—avoid adding more flour, as it will result in dense beignets.

recipe continues

4 Lightly grease the mixing bowl using a few drops of oil, then gather the dough into a ball and place it in the bowl.

5 There are two options for rising the dough, depending on when you want to serve the beignets. To serve them as soon as possible, cover the bowl with a damp kitchen towel and place in a warm spot for 60 minutes to 1½ hours, until the dough doubles in size. Alternatively, to serve the beignets the following day, cover the bowl with plastic and chill in the fridge overnight.

6 Whichever method is used, once the dough has risen, pour the oil into a large, deep saucepan or wide skillet and set over medium-high heat until the temperature reaches 360° to 365°F (182° to 185°C) on a deep-fry thermometer. Cover a heatproof plate with several layers of paper towels and place it near the pan of oil.

7 Transfer the dough to a floured work surface and roll it out until it is ½ inch thick, then cut the dough into 2-inch squares. Carefully place 3 to 4 squares of dough into the hot oil, and cook for 50 to 60 seconds, until golden brown underneath, then flip and cook an additional 50 to 60 seconds. Transfer the beignets to the prepared plate to drain for about 1 minute, then transfer to a serving plate and dust heavily with a thick layer of powdered sugar. Repeat with the remaining squares of dough, adjusting the heat as needed so the oil remains in the correct temperature range. Only cook 3 to 4 beignets at a time, since crowding the pan with too many beignets can cause the oil temperature to drop.

8 Serve warm, with the raspberry coulis for dipping. Bone Appetit!

"In the spring of 1988, I returned to New Orleans, and as soon as I smelled the air, I knew I was home."

—LOUIS DE POINTE DU LAC

"I am the shadow on the moon at night / Filling your dreams to the brim with fright."
—OOGIE BOOGIE

OOGIE BOOGIE OOEY GOOEY GREEN PEANUT BUTTER CHOCOLATE FUDGE

What creature is green, made of a burlap sack crawling with bugs, and has a snake for a tongue? Oogie Boogie, the most frightening resident of Halloween Town. He lives in a dark underground lair with a sadistic collection of torture devices and delights in terrorizing his victims. He even tries to murder Santa Claus by lowering him into a pit of molten lava. While Oogie Boogie might not be the perfect gentleman to bring home to your parents, they'll instantly fall in love after he shares a piece of his homemade fudge. It's ooey, gooey, and loaded with creamy green peanut butter. Swirled with black chocolate fudge to match his sunken eyes, these spooky squares prove that good can be found in everyone, even the Boogie Man.

MAKES 64 SQUARES

- 2 cups (227 g) powdered sugar, divided
- 5 tablespoons (26 g) unsweetened Dutch-process cocoa powder (see Notes)
- 8 tablespoons (1 stick/113 g) unsalted butter, plus more for greasing the baking dish
- 2 cups (426 g) packed dark brown sugar
- ½ cup (118 ml) whole milk
- ¾ teaspoon salt
- 1 cup (270 g) creamy no-stir peanut butter (see Notes)
- 2 teaspoons vanilla extract
- 4 drops black food dye, plus more as needed
- 20 drops green food dye, plus more as needed (see Notes)

1. Grease an 8-inch square baking dish with butter, then line it with a wide piece of parchment paper that covers the entire bottom of the dish and hangs over the sides by an inch or two. This creates a handle to easily lift the fudge out later.

2. In a large mixing bowl, place 1¾ cups (198 g) of the powdered sugar. Set aside.

3. In a small bowl, whisk together the remaining ¼ cup of powdered sugar and the cocoa powder. Set aside.

4. In a medium saucepan, combine the butter, brown sugar, milk, and salt. Set over medium heat and bring to a boil, stirring often. Once the entire mixture is bubbling—not just the edges of the pan—set a timer for 2 minutes and continue to stir. Once the timer rings, remove the pan from heat and quickly stir in the peanut butter and vanilla until smooth and blended.

5. Scoop about ⅔ cup of the peanut butter mixture and pour it into the small bowl of cocoa/powdered sugar. Add the black food dye and stir until blended, adding more color if desired.

6. Add the remaining peanut butter mixture to the large bowl of powdered sugar, and use a hand mixer on medium speed

recipe continues

or stir vigorously until smooth and creamy. Add the green food dye and stir until evenly blended, adding more color, if desired.

7 Pour about half of the green mixture into the prepared baking dish, then scatter dollops of the black mixture over the surface, using about half of the black mixture. Pour in the remaining green mixture, then scatter dollops of the remaining black mixture over the surface. Use a silicone spatula to pat and smooth the surface into an even layer, being careful not to smear the colors. Let the fudge cool at room temperature for 1 hour, then cover and place in the fridge for at least 2 to 3 hours, until chilled.

8 When ready to serve, run a butter knife around the edges of the fudge to loosen the sides, then use the handles to lift the fudge onto a cutting board. Cut into 1-inch squares. Serve chilled or at room temperature. Bone Appetit!

NOTES

Unsweetened cocoa is available in two common types: natural cocoa (which has a reddish-brown color) and Dutch-process (which is almost black). Be sure to use Dutch-process in this recipe for best results.

Be sure to use a no-stir peanut butter. Natural peanut butters contain oils which can result in greasy fudge.

To achieve a bright green color, check craft stores or online for food dyes labeled as "bright green," "leaf green," or "avocado." The green food dye commonly sold in grocery stores is typically a deep shamrock green, which isn't the right hue.

CHOCOLATE MOUSSE DAYDREAM PIE

THE SIXTH SENSE (1999)

Nine-year-old Cole Sear has a difficult time fitting in at school. Arriving home after being bullied by his classmates, his mother tries to raise his spirits by describing a perfect imaginary day where she wins the Pennsylvania lottery, quits her jobs, and spends the afternoon eating chocolate mousse pie in the park. Cole smiles and plays along, bragging that he was picked first for kickball at recess, hit a grand slam to win the game, and was lifted up and carried around as everyone cheered. The next time your day needs a boost, this distracting dessert is a spoonful of happiness. A rich and luxurious chocolate mousse rests on a crispy Oreo cookie crust, topped with clouds of whipped cream and chocolate shavings. Is this the real life? Is this just fantasy? Trust your senses—this heavenly daydream pie is a bit of both!

MAKES ONE 9-INCH PIE

FOR THE CRUST

22 (164 g) Oreo cookies or similar chocolate sandwich cookies

4 tablespoons (½ stick/57 g) unsalted butter, melted

⅛ teaspoon salt

FOR THE FILLING

1⅓ cups (227 g) semisweet chocolate chips

2 cups (473 ml) heavy cream, divided

¼ cup (49 g) granulated sugar

¼ teaspoon salt

2 teaspoons vanilla extract

FOR THE TOPPING

1 cup (237 ml) heavy cream

1 tablespoon granulated sugar

1 teaspoon vanilla extract

Chocolate shavings, for garnish (see Note)

1 Preheat the oven to 350°F (177°C).

2 **MAKE THE CRUST:** Place the Oreo cookies into a food processor and pulse until finely ground and sandy-textured. Transfer the crumbs to a small bowl and add the butter and salt. Stir until the crumbs are evenly moistened, then transfer to a 9-inch pie plate. Spread the mixture and press it into an even layer on the bottom and sides of the plate. Bake for 10 minutes, then place on a wire rack to cool completely.

3 **MAKE THE FILLING:** Fill a medium saucepan with 1 to 2 inches of water and bring to a simmer over medium heat. Place a large heatproof bowl over the pan, so the bottom of the bowl rests above the surface of the simmering water; the bowl should not touch the water. Place the chocolate chips, 1 cup of the heavy cream, the sugar, and salt into the bowl and stir until melted and smooth with no lumps remaining. Carefully remove the hot bowl from the pan, then add the vanilla and stir until blended. Let cool to room temperature, for 30 to 45 minutes.

4 In a large mixing bowl, using an electric mixer, beat the remaining 1 cup of heavy cream on medium-high speed for 3 to 5 minutes, until firm peaks form when the beaters are lifted. Add the whipped cream to the

recipe continues

chocolate mixture and stir gently with a silicone spatula until no streaks remain, being careful not to over-stir and deflate the mousse. Transfer the mixture to the cooled pie crust and spread into an even layer. Cover and chill for at least 4 to 6 hours, or overnight.

5 **MAKE THE TOPPING:** In a large mixing bowl, using an electric mixer, beat the heavy cream on medium-high speed for about 30 seconds, or until foamy, then slowly add the sugar and beat for 3 to 5 minutes, until firm peaks form when the beaters are lifted. Add the vanilla and beat to combine. Spread the whipped cream over the chilled chocolate mousse, then garnish with chocolate shavings. Serve chilled. Bone Appetit!

NOTE

To make chocolate shavings, place a bar of chocolate (the thicker, the better) in the fridge for 15 to 20 minutes to chill. Run a vegetable peeler down the sides of the bar to create curls of chocolate to garnish the pie.

"You know what I did today? I won the Pennsylvania lottery in the morning, I quit my jobs, and I ate a big picnic in the park with lots of chocolate mousse pie."

—LYNN SEAR

"I think a brownie
for breakfast would
fix you right up."
—JET OWENS

BROWNIES FOR BREAKFAST

PRACTICAL MAGIC (1998)

The Owens family of witches, Sally, Gillian, Frances, and Jet, are living the dream. They start each day with chocolate treats, don't bother with silly things like bedtimes or brushing teeth, and consider Midnight Margaritas (page 138) an essential part of their weekly practice. When Gillian returns home after a decade of pursuing abusive relationships, the family welcomes her back with brownies for breakfast. Now you, too, can partake in this ingenious morning ritual. Made with a trio of chocolate—bittersweet, semisweet, and unsweetened—plus a spoonful of coffee crystals, these dark, decadent brownies are rich and fudgy and speckled with chocolate chips. Baked in the evening and chilled overnight, this enchanted breakfast will start the day right.

MAKES 28 TO 32 BROWNIES

- 6 ounces (170 g) 60% bittersweet chocolate, chopped (about 1 cup)
- 2 ounces (57 g) unsweetened chocolate, chopped (about ⅓ cup)
- 12 tablespoons (1½ sticks/170 g) unsalted butter, cubed, plus more softened for greasing the baking dish
- 1 heaping teaspoon instant coffee crystals or instant espresso powder
- 1½ cups (297 g) granulated sugar
- 2 teaspoons vanilla extract
- 1 teaspoon salt
- 4 large eggs, at room temperature
- 1 cup (120 g) all-purpose flour
- 1 cup (170 g) semisweet chocolate chips

1 Preheat the oven to 350°F (177°C). Grease a 9 x 13-inch baking dish with butter, then line it with a wide piece of parchment paper that covers the entire bottom of the dish and hangs over the sides by an inch or two. This creates a handle to easily lift the brownies out later.

2 Fill a medium saucepan with 1 to 2 inches water and bring to a simmer over medium heat. Place a large heatproof bowl over the pan, so the bottom of the bowl rests above the surface of the simmering water, but not touching the water. Place the bittersweet chocolate, unsweetened chocolate, butter, and instant coffee into the bowl and stir until melted and smooth with no lumps remaining. Carefully remove the hot bowl from the pan and set aside to cool for 10 minutes.

3 Once the chocolate has cooled, add the sugar, vanilla, and salt and stir to combine. Add the eggs one at a time, stirring until blended after each addition. Add the flour and stir until no dry streaks remain. Add the chocolate chips and stir until evenly distributed in the dough. Transfer the dough to the prepared baking dish and spread into an even layer. Bake for 25 to 30 minutes, until a toothpick inserted into the center comes out clean with a few moist crumbs sticking to it. Let cool completely in the baking dish for 45 minutes to 1 hour, then cover and refrigerate until chilled, at least 4 hours or preferably overnight.

4 When ready to serve, run a butter knife around the edges of the brownies to loosen the sides, then use the parchment to lift the brownies onto a cutting board. Cut into squares and serve chilled for breakfast. Bone Appetit!

MR. HALLORAN'S HOMEMADE CHOCOLATE ICE CREAM

THE SHINING

(1980)

While Dick Halloran, head chef of the Overlook, gives the new caretakers, Wendy Torrance and her son, Danny, a tour of the hotel's cavernous kitchen, he calls Danny by his family nickname, "Doc," before ever hearing it. He also telepathically asks Danny if he'd like some ice cream as they walk through the aisles of the oversize food pantry. After Wendy leaves with the manager to explore other areas of the Overlook, Dick and Danny discuss their psychic connection over a bowl of chocolate ice cream. Easy to whip up with no machine required, this rich and chocolaty, ultra-simple, no-churn chocolate ice cream shines with flavor. Heeere's chocolate!

MAKES 5 TO 6 CUPS

- 1 (14-ounce/397 g) can sweetened condensed milk
- ½ cup (42 g) unsweetened cocoa powder (see Note)
- 1 tablespoon vanilla extract
- ⅛ teaspoon salt
- 2 cups (473 ml) heavy cream
- Mini semisweet chocolate chips, for garnish (optional)

1. Place a loaf pan in the freezer to chill. In a medium bowl, whisk together the condensed milk, cocoa powder, vanilla, and salt.

2. In a large mixing bowl, using an electric mixer, beat the cream on medium-high speed for 3 to 5 minutes, until firm peaks form when the beaters are lifted. Scoop about 1 cup of the whipped cream into the bowl of chocolate and stir gently with a silicone spatula until evenly combined. Add the remaining whipped cream, and stir gently until no streaks remain, being careful not to over-stir and deflate the cream. Spread the mixture in the chilled loaf pan, and garnish the top with mini chocolate chips, if desired. Freeze for at least 4 to 6 hours. The ice cream can keep in the freezer for up to a month.

NOTE

Cocoa powder is available in two common types: natural cocoa and Dutch-process cocoa. Natural cocoa is reddish-brown, while Dutch-process cocoa is almost black. Either kind will work for this recipe.

"How'd you like some ice cream, Doc?"

—DICK HALLORAN

"Their heads were not found severed.
Their heads were not found at all."
—REVEREND STEENWYCK

HEADLESS GINGERBREAD PEOPLE

SLEEPY HOLLOW
(1999)

In 1799, the quiet village of Sleepy Hollow in upstate New York is rocked by a series of brutal murders. The local townspeople believe the legendary Headless Horseman is to blame, and police detective Ichabod Crane is sent to investigate. All ten of the victims' heads are cleanly severed, as if the killer used a red-hot blade, and none of the heads are ever found. To honor the villagers who lost their lives (and their noggins), these tasty gingerbread people are respectfully decapitated after baking. Made with cinnamon, ginger, cloves, and allspice, our commemorative cookies feature crispy edges, chewy centers, and bloodred icing. Serve these traumatic treats at a *Sleepy Hollow*–themed soirée, and your partygoers will fall head over heels in love.

MAKES 28 TO 32 COOKIES

FOR THE COOKIES

3½ cups (420 g) all-purpose flour, plus more for dusting
1 tablespoon ground ginger
2 teaspoons ground cinnamon
1 teaspoon baking soda
½ teaspoon salt
½ teaspoon ground cloves
½ teaspoon ground allspice
12 tablespoons (1½ sticks/170 g) unsalted butter, at room temperature
¾ cup (160 g) packed dark brown sugar
1 large egg, at room temperature
¾ cup (255 g) molasses
1 teaspoon vanilla extract

FOR THE ICING

2 cups (226 g) powdered sugar
2 teaspoons light corn syrup
2 tablespoons plus 2 teaspoons whole milk
½ teaspoon vanilla extract
Red food dye
Additional food dyes in the colors of choice (optional)

1 **MAKE THE COOKIES:** In a small bowl, whisk together the flour, ginger, cinnamon, baking soda, salt, cloves, and allspice. Set aside.

2 In a large mixing bowl, using an electric mixer, beat the butter and brown sugar on medium speed until light and fluffy. Add the egg, molasses, and vanilla and beat until smooth. Add the flour mixture and beat until no dry streaks remain. Gather the dough, then divide in half. Roll each half into a ball, wrap tightly in plastic wrap, then flatten slightly to make a disc shape and refrigerate for at least 2 hours. The dough can keep in the fridge for up to 1 week.

3 To bake the cookies, preheat the oven to 350°F (177°C).

4 Since this dough is fairly sticky, it is best to roll it between two sheets of parchment paper. First, place a 16-inch square of parchment on the countertop and lightly dust it with flour. Unwrap one of the discs of dough, place it in the center of the parchment, and lightly dust the top of the dough with flour. Place another 16-inch square of

recipe continues

parchment on top of the dough and use a rolling pin to flatten the dough between the two pieces of parchment until it makes a large circle approximately ¼ inch thick. If the dough begins to stick to the parchment while rolling, lift the parchment and dust the dough with flour before continuing. Once the dough is rolled ¼ inch thick, use the parchment to lift the flattened circle of dough onto a baking sheet. Place the baking sheet in the freezer for 15 minutes; this will firm up the dough and ensures clean cutout shapes. Repeat the process with the second disc of dough.

5 Remove the baking sheets from the freezer and use the parchment to lift the dough onto the countertop. Using a person-shaped cookie cutter, cut out as many shapes as possible, dipping the cookie cutter in flour between cuts to prevent sticking, if needed. Transfer the cookies to a parchment-lined baking sheet, leaving about 1 inch of space between each one. Repeat with the second circle of dough. Gather and reroll the dough scraps, then cut out the remaining cookies, using additional baking sheets as needed. Place the baking sheets in the freezer for 15 minutes; this helps the cookies keep their shape while baking.

6 Transfer the baking sheets directly to the oven and bake for 9 to 11 minutes, until the edges of the cookies begin to darken slightly and the centers no longer appear wet. If baking two sheets at once, swap the positions of the baking sheets halfway through to ensure the cookies bake evenly. Let the cookies cool on the baking sheet for 5 minutes, then transfer to a wire rack to cool completely, about 20 minutes.

7 **MAKE THE ICING:** In a small bowl, stir together the powdered sugar, corn syrup, milk, and vanilla until smooth and blended. The texture of the icing should be thick enough so that when you drizzle a spoonful of icing into the bowl, it holds its shape for a moment before dissolving. Set aside a small portion of the icing in a separate bowl and tint it red. The remaining icing can remain white, or if using additional colors, divide it into small bowls and tint each one the color of your choice.

8 Transfer each color of icing to a piping bag fitted with a small round tip, or a zip-top bag with the corner cut off.

9 Use a sharp knife to cut off the heads from each gingerbread person, then decorate the severed necks with red icing. Using additional colors, decorate the heads and bodies to your liking. The icing will dry in 20 to 30 minutes. Bone Appetit!

VERY CHERRY MINI TARTS

THE WITCHES OF EASTWICK (1987)

Felicia Alden, the nosy town gossip, is appalled that her new neighbor, Daryl Van Horne, is living with three girlfriends, Alex, Jane, and Sukie. Felicia spitefully tries to ruin their reputations by spreading malicious rumors, even interrupting a Sunday church service to publicly shame them. Her cruel actions come back to haunt her when Daryl casts an evil spell, causing millions of cherry pits to violently erupt from her mouth like a geyser. Just when you thought you'd never want to see a cherry again, these mini tarts will change your mind. Flaky, buttery, and bursting with a profusion of cherries—revenge has never tasted better.

MAKES 8 MINI TARTS

FOR THE FILLING

5 cups (655 g) pitted cherries, fresh or frozen

¾ cup (149 g) granulated sugar

½ cup (118 ml) water

¼ cup (30 g) cornstarch

2 tablespoons freshly squeezed lemon juice

⅛ teaspoon salt

⅛ teaspoon ground cinnamon

1 teaspoon vanilla extract

FOR THE CRUST (SEE NOTE)

2½ cups (300 g) all-purpose flour, plus more for dusting

2 tablespoons granulated sugar

1 teaspoon salt

16 tablespoons (2 sticks/227 g) cold unsalted butter, cubed

½ cup (118 ml) ice water

⅛ teaspoon almond extract

Whipped cream, homemade (see page 183) or store-bought, for garnish

Fresh mint leaves, for garnish (optional)

1 **MAKE THE FILLING:** In a medium saucepan, combine the fresh cherries, sugar, water, cornstarch, lemon juice, salt, and cinnamon. Bring to a simmer over medium heat, stirring often, then reduce the heat to low and simmer for 6 to 8 minutes, until the mixture has thickened and the cherries have softened. Remove from the heat, then add the vanilla and stir to combine. Let cool to room temperature, then use immediately or transfer to a sealed container and store in the fridge for up to 3 days.

2 **MAKE THE CRUST:** In a large mixing bowl, whisk together the flour, sugar, and salt until evenly combined. Add the butter and use a pastry blender or two knives to work the butter into the flour until the largest pieces are the size of peanuts. Add the ice water and the almond extract and stir until the dough begins to clump together. Briefly work it with your hands, gathering it together into one ball without over-kneading the dough. If it is too dry and not holding together, add more ice water 1 teaspoon at a time until it is moist enough to gather into one ball. Cut the dough in half, roll each half into a ball, then wrap each one tightly in plastic wrap, pressing it into a disc shape. Refrigerate for at least 30 minutes, or up to 1 day.

3 To bake the tarts, preheat the oven to 400°F (204°C).

4 Remove one of the chilled discs of dough from the refrigerator, unwrap it, and place on a floured work surface. Roll out the dough until it is ¼ inch thick. Place a 4-inch tart pan

recipe continues

upside down on the dough and use a pastry cutter or knife to cut a circle around the edge of the tart pan. Cut out as many circles as possible from the dough. Place each dough circle into a 4-inch tart pan with a removable bottom, pressing it gently into the bottom and sides of the pan. Repeat with the second disc of dough, until all eight tart pans are filled. Cover each tart crust with a square of parchment paper and fill it with ceramic pie weights or dried beans, to keep the crust from puffing up as it bakes.

5 Transfer the tarts to a rimmed baking sheet and place in the freezer for 10 minutes.

6 Transfer the baking sheet directly to the oven and bake for 16 to 18 minutes, until golden. Let the tarts cool on the pan for 5 minutes, then remove the weights and transfer the tart pans to a wire rack to cool completely, 20 to 25 minutes.

7 To serve, remove the tart crusts from the pans. Place a generous layer of cherry filling over each tart crust and garnish with a dollop of whipped cream and, if desired, a mint leaf. Serve at room temperature or chilled. Bone Appetit!

NOTE

To save time, feel free to use a store-bought pie crust.

**“Don’t let her get to you.
Have a cherry.”**

—DARYL VAN HORNE

ACKNOWLEDGMENTS

To our coven of family and friends, for your eternal love and support. We couldn't have crafted these spells without you. To Leigh Eisenman, for being the best literary agent in the biz. Honored to have worked with you since 2016. Cheers to many more fun projects together and cocktail dates in the city. To Ronnie Alvarado, for coming up with the brilliant idea for this book! It's been so fun bringing this project to life—or perhaps raising it from the dead? Thank you for your friendship and impeccable editing skills. To Rachel Saltzman, our high priestess and manager since the beginning of time. To Lauren Volo, for your gorgeous photography and lighting wizardry. Can we do this again please? To Mira Evnine, for your magic hands and supernatural food styling skills. Thanks for the killer playlists and witty conversation. To Maeve Sheridan, for your imagination, creativity, and wicked props! Thanks for helping make this book look so bloody amazing. To Debbie Kim, for preparing sixty-five recipes in six days. Thanks for making the process feel so smooth and easy. To Geordeen Chambers, Stacy La, Fabi Arce, and Zach Molina, thanks for being part of our coven and for helping out at the studio. To everyone who has supported us over the years on our blog and on social media and has made our recipes at home. Thank you!

Corrections page—We thought it would be helpful to add a page on our website that will list any corrections or clarifications for this book. You can find it at www.husbandsthatcook.com/whoops. There is a place to comment, so please let us know if you find any typos in these pages.

Website—Visit us at www.husbandsthatcook.com and sign up for our email list to stay up-to-date with more Husbands' recipes and all the latest news. Come say hello and let us know if you have any questions or comments—we would love to hear from you!

Social media—We can't wait to see what you make from the book, so use the hashtag #HalloweenMovieCookbook and tag @husbandsthatcook on social media so we can see your creations.

INDEX

NOTE: Page references in *italics* refer to photos of recipes. References to individual Halloween movie titles include pages with corresponding recipes and the recipe photos.

D

E

F

G

H

S

ABOUT THE AUTHORS

Ryan Alvarez and Adam Merrin are two husbands that cook together in a small kitchen in a house on a hill in Eagle Rock, California.

They met in 2001 in a recording studio where Ryan was singing with a jazz choir and Adam was the engineer. They fell in love, and five years later were married. Since its inception in 2015, their blog, *Husbands That Cook*, was a finalist for *Saveur* magazine's Best How-To Cooking Blog Award and a Taste Talks Awards Nominee for Best Food Blog. Their self-titled debut cookbook, *Husbands That Cook* (March 2019, St. Martin's Press), is filled with more than 130 inventive vegetarian recipes, vibrant photos, and stories about their relationship. Their second cookbook, *That Takes the Cookie* (November 2024, S&S/Simon Element), offers delicious cookie recipes for every occasion, all year round. When Ryan and Adam are not cooking, they love being in nature, hiking, and spending time in their garden. Adam is also a musician and one of the founding members of indie rock band The 88. Ryan sings classical music and acts in TV shows and commercials. Visit www.husbandsthatcook.com to learn more.

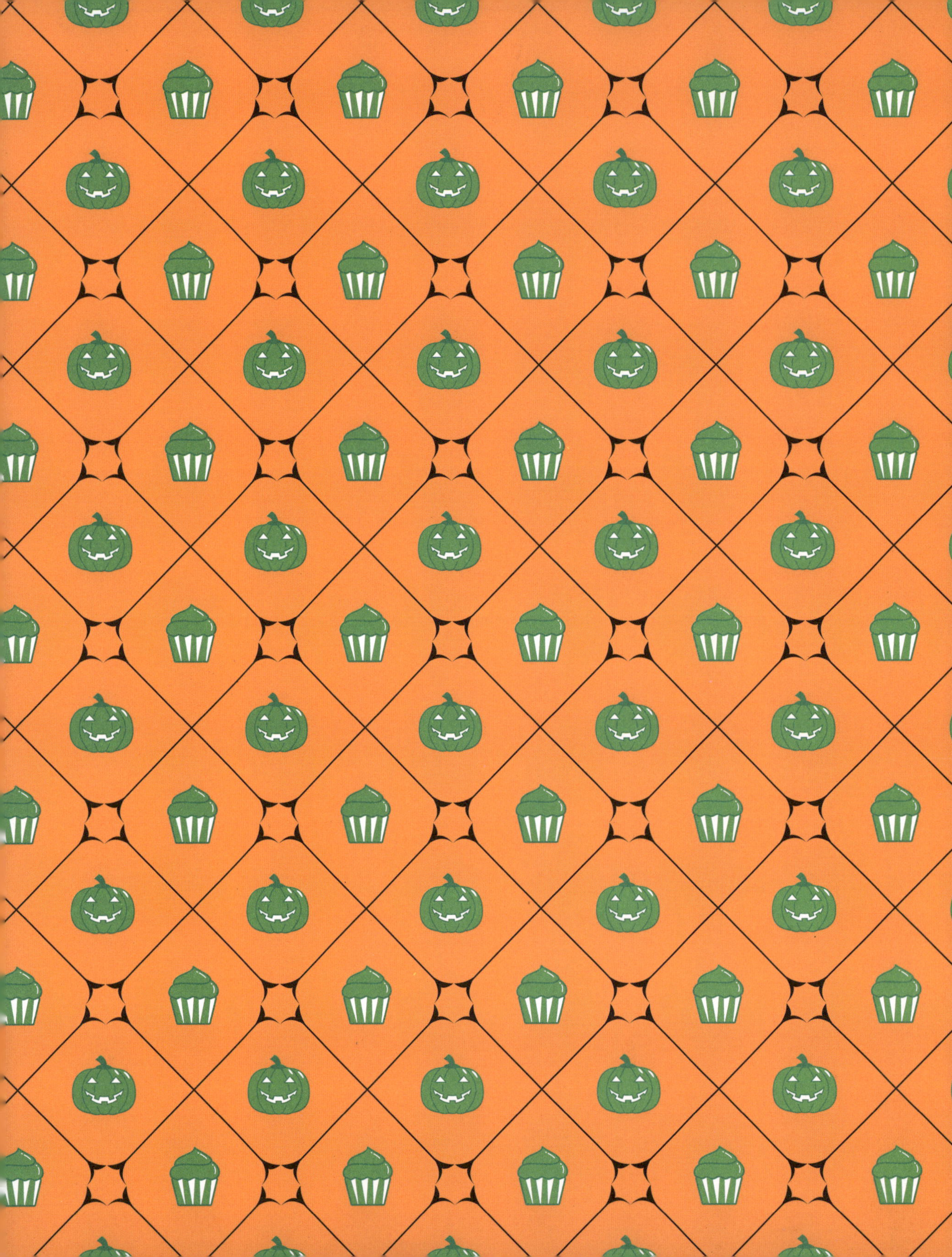